THE GARRISON GAME

The
Garrison
Game

The State of Irish Football

Dave Hannigan

MAINSTREAM
PUBLISHING

EDINBURGH AND LONDON

*For my mother, Theresa, my father, Denis, and
my wife, Cathy*

First published in Great Britain in 1998 by
MAINSTREAM PUBLISHING COMPANY (EDINBURGH) LTD
7 Albany Street
Edinburgh EH1 3UG

ISBN 1 85158 980 5

A catalogue record for this book is available from the British Library

Typeset in Cheltenham
Printed and bound in Great Britain by Butler and Tanner Ltd

Contents

Acknowledgements and explanations

This book doesn't contain a chapter dealing with the game in Northern Ireland because I felt that the subject matter deserves and requires a book all of its own. Apologies as well to the purists who say the term 'soccer' is an aberration. I have used 'soccer' and 'football' interchangeably in the book because in the course of interviews with people of different generations, I found that this was common practice.

Those out of the way, I would like to thank the following for giving of their time for this book: Joe Fitzpatrick, Brendan Menton Snr, Eamon Dunphy, Noel Griffin, Noel McCabe, Pat Devlin, John Freeman, Kieron O'Regan, John Donegan, Maurice McCrohan, Tony Booth, Peter Carbery, Murt Murphy, Plunkett Carter, Maire Rua Gallagher, Liam Tuohy, Davy Langan, Declan Field and his family. I am especially grateful to Brian Kerr and Pat Dolan for accommodating me, even though I have insulted their great work at Saint Patrick's Athletic in the past.

Most of the quotes used in the Roy Keane chapter are taken from the RTE television documentary on his life, 'Have Boots, Will Travel', on which I collaborated with Colm O'Callaghan, a man whose innate sense of Cork was always a great help.

A particular debt is owing as well to Bob Hennessy, a

wonderful journalist and an obliging friend, and to Denis Walsh and Paul Howard who were an inestimable help in the initial editing stage; it has been a privilege to work and drink with them both.

Many others didn't contribute directly to this book but deserve a mention for the assistance they have given me through the years; namely Tony Connolly, Frank O'Sullivan, John Bowen, Georgie Scanlon, Jamesie Wilson, Liam McCarthy, Kevin O'Halloran, John O'Halloran, Gavin O'Connor, Ciaran Spillane, Keith Cooney, Deirdre McCarthy, Mark Penney, Mark O'Loughlin, Gus Roche, Ken Cotter, Emmet Barry, Gary Murphy, Jed Kelly, Ger Siggins, Paul Kimmage and Guy Sarfati.

Thanks to Bill Campbell for being the only publisher who would ring somebody back on a Sunday, and to Andrea Fraile for such a fine and patient editing job.

I would also like to pay special tribute to my mother and father, my sisters Anne and Denise, and my brother Tom for everything they have given me.

Finally, this book would not have been possible without the love, patience and understanding of Cathy Frost. There are no words to express my gratitude to her.

If I have forgotten anybody, I apologise now. And all of the mistakes are of course, my own.

Prologue

My mother's father, Tommy Morrissey, played for Cork United in the '40s. He handed one of his jerseys down to me and my brother Tom. Predominantly red, with a round, white collar of the type that has lately become fashionable again, the fabric was heavy and almost hairy to the touch. Our mother shrunk it in the wash but that jersey made us believe every one of his stories about the verbal abuse he received when hugging the left wing down the 'Dyke. ' "I've seen a better pair of wings on a duck," was what some smart alec shouted,' he told us, chuckling.

My father broke his ankle once in a caravan park in Garretstown, following an abortive attempt to show his kids how to perform the Johann Cruyff drag-back. He loved that Holland team, and for Christmas one year, he gave us both an orange football, a Johann Cruyff football. He swore to us that Wim Van Hanegem was one of our Dutch cousins, that Germans couldn't be trusted after the great injustice of 1974, and that *Shoot* was better for us than *Roy of the Rovers*. Two out of three wasn't bad.

Introduction

'There'll be no garrison games for Ireland. These only aid the
peaceful penetration of Ireland by the British
and there should be no soccer for Gaels'
MICHAEL COLLINS, 1908

I

The Garrison Game. The phrase, like the above quote,
belongs in a history book. Nobody really calls it that
anymore. Maybe occasionally, an anti-soccer fundamen-
talist might use the term. Most likely, he'd have to explain it
to anybody within earshot who was under the age of 20. The
garrison towns were those which housed British Army
bases, where the soldiers and their children could be seen
playing British games. In order of importance, the garrison
games were soccer, rugby and cricket, and while these
towns generally remain hotbeds of soccer support, they
have been superseded by so many other townlands and
villages in this passion that the term no longer means
anything.

Bertie Ahern is Taoiseach of Ireland and leader of Fianna
Fáil, a party which enunciates its policy towards Irishness
as follows: 'Fianna Fáil represents people who have a pride
in their country, people who are not always denigrating our
achievements, our values and our outlook. Our legislation

should reflect our own needs, and the type of society that we want, not just import the norms that apply elsewhere. The very purpose of national independence is that it allows us to do things differently in our own way.'

On first name terms with Alex Ferguson, Ahern is also the most famous Manchester United supporter in the country. In December, 1994, he penned an article for *The Sunday Tribune* in which he paid due homage. Under the heading 'Why I love Man United – Ahern' he wrote: 'I must confess to being a life-long supporter of that much maligned institution, Manchester United FC. My affection for United dates back to my earliest days when, as a young lad kicking a ball around on the streets of Drumcondra, I used to pretend to be Liam Whelan.

'There always seemed to be an Irish connection at United... I was always impressed by Sir Matt Busby. He was a charismatic and dignified figure and gave the impression of being a genial, fatherly type. He was a devout Catholic and United were considered to be a Catholic club, which is another reason Irish people identified with them.'

His devotion to all things Old Trafford serves, if anything, to underline just how ordinary a person Ahern actually is. In the Dublin streets where he grew up in the '50s and '60s, a lot of kids would have aspired to emulate the achievements of Liam Whelan and, later, Johnny Giles, by one day playing for Manchester United. When the vast majority realised that this was beyond them, they sated their desires by supporting the team. That Ahern's other great sporting love is the Dublin Gaelic footballers only makes him typical of the genre.

At the peak of their success in the mid-'70s, the Dublin Gaelic footballers attracted such an enormous, colourful following that they were described as the Manchester United of the Gaelic Athletic Association (GAA). More than 20 years later, the Gaelic football analyst Colm O'Rourke explained the role that Glen Ryan was playing during a championship match between Dublin and Kildare by saying that he was operating as 'a sweeper'. O'Rourke, one of the greatest players of the modern era, has attended Serie A and

Premiership soccer matches, and would be familiar with the language of the other game. He is not alone in this.

In Ireland, the sports fan is a much more fluid and less bigoted individual than he used to be and there is no more potent example of this than in Cork. Many of the people who swelled Cork City's crowds to more than twice their normal size during their run to victory in the 1998 FAI Cup final are the same ones who, come the summer, support the county's Gaelic football and hurling teams in the championship. Of course, there is still some mutual exclusion and there always will be, but not as much as narrow-minded people would have us believe. The average sports fan is usually just that – a fan of sports and the Irish of the species just have more to choose from than most.

There are many ways to illustrate the Irish obsession with the British game. This attempt begins 3,000 miles from Ireland, in Brighton, Massachussetts. In The Green Briar, a bar with a largely Irish clientèle, there is a stack of newsletters on a stand by the phones out back. *The Irish Emigrant* stares at passers-by, distinguished by the green paper on which it is printed. The colour of the paper is designed to make it stand out or, some say, to reflect its politics. In any case, it is what its subhead proclaims it to be – 'The week's news and sports: direct from Ireland.' Its 52 pages contain a neat précis of news from home, mixed in with advertisements relevant to the huge expatriate community all along America's north-eastern seaboard.

But the week's sport from Ireland includes three pages of Premiership news. Three pages, and this from a sample edition taken in the last week of July, 1997, a full fortnight before the English season proper had begun. The reports are a mix of transfer news: Paul Ince's signing for Liverpool, David Ginola moving from Newcastle United to Spurs, and other snippets such as quotes from Alex Ferguson's latest diary of a season. This swathe of British soccer news co-exists with details about Gaelic football and hurling matches from Ireland.

Why then does a newsletter, the purpose of which is to provide a link with home for its emigrant readership, contain a huge chunk of English and Scottish soccer news? Because that is what its readers want. Keeping abreast of the exploits of your favourite team is an integral bond with home. The vast majority of Irish youngsters grow up supporting a particular English club or Celtic, and though maturity and distance may diminish their passion, there is still an attachment there. The editorial content of *The Irish Emigrant* merely reflects what its readers want to see and there is further evidence of this in its advertisements.

Boston is a city with a seemingly infinite number of Irish pubs, so the competition for business is particularly fierce and the ads taken out by the various bars reflect this. Everything from free parking to free bands are used to lure people in. But in among all the 'Traditional Irish Seissun [*sic*] every Thursday', and 'Live Irish music nightly', there are enticements such as live hurling and Gaelic football matches from Ireland. Then there's the foreign game.

Bad Abbot's Irish pub is unequivocal. 'Soccer coming soon', its ad reads. 'The Umbro Cup, the Charity Shield and the Premier League.' The Plough and the Stars offers 'English league soccer, every Saturday and Sunday.' The bar staff will vouch that the people who file in on Saturday mornings for the Premiership are back on Sunday mornings for the hurling and Gaelic football.

One more strange fact about the audiences watching Premiership soccer in Irish pubs all along the east coast of America is that very often, members of the Republican sympathisers' group Noraid, are seen actively – and voluntarily – cheering their favourite English clubs. In their other guise, these people spend their time campaigning to get 'the Brits' out of Ireland. One more cogent illustration of the bizarreness of Ireland's relationship with British soccer.

The American publicans are only catering for their customers' needs and in this they are not alone. In a suburban Dublin pub on a Saturday afternoon, maybe 100 people are gathered in front of two televisions, anticipating live pictures direct from Filbert Street as Leicester City are about to take on Liverpool. Nothing unusual there. Any decent Premiership match attracts good crowds to Irish pubs. But Sky Sports don't show live football on Saturday afternoons, and the national broadcaster, RTE, is prohibited from doing so. Just before 3 p.m. with the pictures showing players limbering up for kick-off, a barman reaches for the volume button and all is revealed: the commentary is entirely in Norwegian. What we are watching here is what is being beamed into Scandinavian homes every weekend.

This scene is being replicated in towns all over Ireland, and in this particular corner of south Dublin, nobody seems to care about the language barrier. For 90 minutes, the fans are enraptured. That they cannot understand a word of what the commentator is saying doesn't detract from their enjoyment of the game. Now and then they burst into laughter at the strange phonation of the foreign language. For example, Steve McManaman dribbling with the ball sounds something like: 'Hurdy, hurdy, hurdy, hurdy, McManaman.' The scene could be straight out of *Father Ted*, and as one wag puts it: 'It must be the chef from *The Muppets* who's doing the commentary.'

The strange tongue hardly matters a jot otherwise. The regulars are even able to decipher the meaning of the Norwegian phrases which periodically flash up on the screen, accompanying the scores from other games. They know that 'Arsenal 1 Sheff Wed 0 (Slutt)' translates as a full-time result, that 'straffe' means penalty and 'asmal' is the Norwegian for own goal. Football as the universal language, sort of. In any case, nobody leaves before the final whistle, and on the way out, a chalk scrawl on a blackboard by the door reminds them: 'Live Premiership football, every Saturday.'

Nobody is absolutely certain about the legal status of using satellites to broadcast Norwegian football in Irish pubs, but for now, most pubs that have opted for the Norwegian route have kept with it because they realise that there is an insatiable hunger for Premiership football in this country. That the public are willing to watch games where the commentary is exclusively in Norwegian is ample proof of that, even if the number of times that the pub drunk shouts out: 'Jeez, that Andy Gray sounds a bit ropey today,' can become annoying after a while.

The businessmen behind the provision of the technology required to tap into the Scandinavian signal are not the only astute movers to realise the commercial sense in expanding the diet of televised soccer in Ireland. When Teilifis na Gaeilge went on air in October 1996, its expressed aim was the promotion and preservation of our native language and culture. A much criticised entity even before its inception, TnaG was anxious to do whatever it could to get people watching the station.

With this in mind, an independent production company was commissioned to come up with a soccer highlights programme. Having toyed with the idea of broadcasting the National League of Ireland, and then the Brazilian championship, they finally settled on the Spanish Liga A. After a while, a Scottish highlights segment was incorporated into the programme they christened 'Ole, Ole', and every Monday night, the show attracts up to 100,000 viewers, a figure large enough to regularly place it in the top three TnaG transmissions.

Again, there is a touch of the surreal in all this. Apart from hearing of the exploits of Messrs Luis Figo, Rivaldo, Clarence Seedorf and Co described mellifluously in the Irish tongue, we then listen to the post-match interviews: Jupp Heycknes, behind a podium, mouthing Spanish phrases with subtitles in Irish running underneath. Formulated, produced and packaged from a facility in the Ring Gaeltacht, County Waterford, 'Ole, Ole' gets people watching TnaG who don't normally tune in and the station bosses are satisfied they are on to a winner.

'There's no doubt that the majority of people watching our programme are not living in the Gaeltacht but in urban areas dotted around the country. We find a lot of pubs in Dublin put it on as a curtain-raiser before the Monday night football on Sky Sports,' says presenter/producer Micheal O'Domhnaill.

There have even been reports that in the loyalist enclaves along Belfast's Shankhill Road, Rangers fans have been tapping into the RTE signal to watch highlights of games which are only otherwise available to them on Sky Sports.

That Irish is the official language of Republicanism only adds to the irony of all this.

'Even the bastions of loyalist Belfast have been penetrated through the medium of TnaG,' wrote Roddy Forsyth in *The Title* newspaper. 'TnaG guarantees a fix of Rangers' games more frequently that can be supplied by the satellite broadcasters. So although it is usually anathema for locals to put tongue to Erse, they are quite prepared to accommodate Micheal O'Domhnaill introducing the Gers in Gaelic.'

TnaG further sates the appetite of soccer fans with a series called *World Cup Gold*. Introduced by the former Republic of Ireland goalkeeper Packie Bonner, each programme replays in full a World Cup game from a past competition. The commentary is entirely in English with the ads in between the only concession to the Irish language. Although the re-showing of games from the Charlton era has only underlined the poor quality of many of the matches involving his team, *World Cup Gold* has still been a resounding success.

Dublin Airport, 6.45 a.m., 14 March 1998. In less than five hours, Manchester United play Arsenal in one of those games that kicks off ludicrously early at the behest of Sky Sports. The departure lounge is thronged with football supporters. Not your regular English, shirts-open, lager-lout, shouting-at-the-top-of-their-voices supporters. These are a more mundane bunch. There are husband and wife teams, fathers and sons. Even the 20-somethings who might fit most easily into the stereotypical view of a football fan are uncommonly well behaved, opting to leaf through the morning papers rather than unnerve passers-by.

Once upon a time in the not so distant past, Irish supporters travelled to England overnight by boat on the Friday. Crossings were often rough and conditions were difficult, but that only added to the romance of it all. However, the introduction of extensive flights to England by Ryanair in the early 1990s lowered the price of air travel and meant that the Irish soccer fan had a new alternative.

Instead of arriving in Manchester at dawn on Saturday morning, and passing time in places like the *Coronation Street* Tour in Granada Studios, they could now arrive in Manchester around midday and make their way to Old Trafford at their leisure.

On the night that Manchester United were knocked out of the Champions' League by Monaco, there were seven extra Ireland-bound flights laid on. Factoring in the scheduled flights that would have been carrying Irish fans home all through the next day, it is fair to surmise that there were maybe 2,000 Irish at the game.

The willingness of the Irish soccer supporters to travel in such massive contingents to games in England and Scotland is the root cause of the plans to relocate Wimbledon and Clydebank to Dublin. Whatever the moral standing of these proposals, the thinking behind them is based on simple and apparently sound business principles. As Paul McGuinness, the manager of U2, put it during his involvement with the scheme: 'Dublin is an audience without a team, Wimbledon is a team without an audience.'

The appetite for Premiership football appears to be growing, and it's significant that no Irish travel agent ever has trouble getting tickets for the big games in England, with Manchester United deemed the most accommodating in this respect. Old Trafford's 55,000 capacity helps in this regard, so does the way in which the fans conduct themselves. Clever marketing people that they are, Manchester United PLC realise, too, that a day-tripper from Ireland will spend more, much more, in the super- and megastores than a fan who sees a dozen games a year. Not only will the Irish fan be buying for himself, and maybe his own children, but he will also have been given money from his next door neighbour or his friend from work to buy on their behalf too.

The relatively easy availability of tickets for Irish fans, and other day-trippers, has annoyed die-hard United fans. They blame the atmosphere deterioration on the non-regulars and consider it as being one more reason to dislike the PLC. Yet, it has been pointed out that it is the Irish fans, and perhaps their Scandinavian counterparts who make the Manchester United merchandising operation so profitable and allow them, now and again, to splash out on an Andy Cole, a Roy Keane or a Jaap Stam. They can't have it both ways and, in any case, Ireland's passion for the Premiership in general and Manchester United in particular remains undiminished by such carping.

The other side of this is that the Premiership allegiances often obscure people's sense of reality. For years now, it has been commonplace at pre-season friendlies for English glamour teams to be cheered more than the Irish club that are hosting their visit to these parts. This curious tendency received its weirdest expression to date in May of this year when the Irish Under-16 team was introduced to the crowd at half-time in a friendly international between Ireland and Mexico at Lansdowne Road.

A dreadfully dull afternoon was enlivened no end by the presence of the squad which had recently won the European Championships. But the presentation of the first Irish soccer team to win a major trophy at any level was marred by the crowd booing three of the players, Kevin Grogan, Graham Barrett and David McMahon. The trio's crime consisted of being young apprentices at Manchester United, Arsenal and Newcastle respectively, and the finest achievement of their young lives was temporarily blighted by Irish supporters intent on voicing their allegiance to an English club side. There is no more graphic illustration of the dichotomy that is Ireland's strange, ill-defined relationship with the professional game in Britain.

II

On a Sunday morning in the summer of 1996, Denis Irwin walked the short distance from his mother's house in Togher, Cork, to the local GAA club, St Finnbarr's. For Irwin, it was a routine journey, one he has made at least once every close-season since he first departed Cork for an apprenticeship with Leeds United 15 years earlier. Once in the grounds, he stopped a while to take in a street league match, a competition between rival neighbourhoods, which he himself played in 20 or so years before.

Shortly after his arrival, two of the youngsters on the field recognised the face, and neglecting their stations, ran towards him. Once the rest of the players caught wind of just who was watching, the game was temporarily abandoned as Irwin found himself surrounded by more than 30 ten-year-olds. Before normal service could resume, Irwin had to agree to stay and watch the entire game. After the match had ended, he stood in goal and every player on the field took a penalty shot against him. Then they allowed him to go home.

Irwin, the man about whom Alex Ferguson loved to say: 'You can put the kettle on by Denis' doesn't rank as the most glamorous member of the team of the decade, yet this is the effect he can have on ten-year-olds. An illustration of the inroads which television and the Premiership have made into the hearts and minds of Irish children, or a sort of home-coming for a local boy who made good? Cork city has always been such a fecund region for sport in general and soccer in particular, that there is probably merit in both views. In other counties though, the situation is more clear-cut.

There was no such thing as organised soccer in Kerry before 1971. The existence of Rule 27 in the GAA Official Guide, which imposed an automatic suspension on a member playing, attending or promoting, soccer, rugby, hockey and cricket, effectively stunted any attempts to do so. A team from Tralee did spend the '60s playing in the Desmond League all right, their experience replete with apocryphal tales of players donning wigs to dodge the Damocletian implications of the Ban, and goalposts getting cut down in the night. Once the Ban was lifted, however, soccer in Kerry came out of the closet.

A representative of the Munster Football Association travelled down to Tralee one night in 1971. A meeting was held, lit by candles and a pilly lamp, by the side of the Low Field in the town, and a Kerry league of eight clubs was sanctioned. There are 3,000 registered players in the county now – a whopping 2,000 more than there were only ten years ago.

Some day soon, Niall Hobbert, an 18-year-old goalkeeper from Tralee Dynamos, will sign for some English club or other (at least three are interested) and become Kerry's first professional soccer player ever. It won't be long then until the National League of Ireland grant membership to an application from a Kerry club. Determined to be first in the queue, Tralee Dynamos, currently in the Munster Senior League, have already appointed a full-time commercial manager.

At the other end of the scale, Club Smerbhic, a team from the western-most tip of the Kerry Gaeltacht, are in their third season in junior soccer. Local aficionado Murt Murphy reckons there are a number of factors behind the extraordinary growth. 'The prominence of the international team and Manchester United obviously enough, but soccer has also been helped by the barren years of Gaelic football in the county between 1986 and 1997.'

Twenty-five years ago, in his autobiography, *A Kerry Footballer*, Mick O'Connell wrote:

> *'In the immediate future, I cannot see the game [soccer] making much progress in Ireland because of the poor condition of the pitches and the lack of good soccer to watch. The majority of the pitches are bumpy enough to baffle Pele himself and young players, especially those in rural areas, never actually see good players, and to learn this game properly this is a necessity. They can read all the books on the bookshelves, see all the World Cup matches in the world on television, but these are very poor substitutes for the real thing, a sideline view of good football.'*

O'Connell was the greatest exponent of Gaelic football ever, but he was badly wrong about the boon television, and especially the advent of satellite, would bring soccer. As the level of TV coverage increased gradually throughout the

'80s and '90s, so too did the number of homes into which the English, and eventually the extra-terrestrial stations, were being beamed. With the improved and cheaper technology, more and more people in the remotest corners of Ireland were getting to see more and more soccer and there could only be one end result. In May 1998, Tralee Dynamos won the FAI Youths Cup by beating Stella Maris, one of the most famous and long-established Dublin nurseries.

Murt Murphy is quick to point out, too, though, that for all the boom, the majority of soccer clubs in Kerry co-exist peacefully with their GAA counterparts. Even the sour aftertaste of the ban that infected some is gone at this stage. The restricted numbers available often mean that rural clubs from the different codes are drawing their players from the same pool, and co-operation between fixtures secretaries is common enough to be unremarkable.

In this respect, Kerry is a model of what's happening all over the rest of the country. For the reasons Murt Murphy cites, soccer has exploded in nearly every county during the last decade. The blossoming has not only been confined to places like Cork, Donegal, Sligo, Waterford, where it has always thrived, or indeed, Dublin, the hub of the game in this country. Roscommon, Mayo and Wexford all report massive increases in the numbers playing the game.

The situation in Wexford actually replicates that in Kerry. The county hurling team's lack of success throughout the '70s, '80s and half of the '90s left a void in the imagination of youngsters which was so effectively colonised by televised soccer that, in a 1995 survey of schoolchildren, soccer headed the poll as most popular sport, with Eric Cantona deemed the most popular sportsman. Moreover, there were 17 soccer players in the list of top 25 favourite sportspersons as opposed to just one hurler.

The county's subsequent All Ireland hurling success in 1996 was rightly pounced upon by GAA people to start the fightback. Liam Griffin, the instigator of the triumph and perhaps hurling's most eloquent evangelist delivered several impassioned speeches on his game's behalf.

Speaking to one set of schoolchildren after his team's victory, he said:

'How many of you will play for Liverpool or for Manchester United? How many of you could reasonably expect even to play for Huddersfield Town? You can't even aspire to that. But many of you could realistically play in Croke Park for Wexford. That's real. That's something worth aiming for. It's a great game, our game. Not a plastic far-away unrealisable dream. Look at Billy Byrne and compare him to Gazza. Billy plays for the honour of his county. Unpaid and unspoiled, a man who has given his life to bring pride back to the place of his birth. Gazza is an asshole. When you go home tonight, put on your Newcastle Brown Ale shirt and take a good look in the mirror. Then take it off and put on your purple and gold jersey and look again. Ask yourself: "Which one am I?" The answer should be obvious.'

Undoubtedly, Griffin's munificent oratory on the game's behalf will have long-reaching effects on soccer in that county, but for now, both codes are getting on fine. In the same month that the Wexford hurlers were ending a 28-year famine with their All Ireland final triumph over Limerick, another division was added to the county junior soccer league. That took the number in total to nine.

Schoolboy soccer is in such rude health in Wexford that it can no longer admit new teams. As things stand already, the demand on pitches is so great that in the winter months, most schoolboy teams only get to play every second weekend. Paddy Fitzpatrick is currently on the books of Glasgow Celtic, while five of his fellow countymen are under constant surveillance by English clubs. Despite Liam Griffin's assertions of the degree of difficulty involved in making it as a professional, more will definitely follow.

Across the border in Kilkenny, even if nobody has made the jump cross-channel yet, the day when somebody does is coming soon. In March 1998, St Kieran's College, Ireland's foremost hurling academy, were beaten in the final of the

Leinster Schools' senior soccer competition by St Joseph's Fairview, a Dublin school which used to be renowned for its Gaelic football teams. St Kieran's had won the cup in 1993, an unremarkable feat in the greater scheme of things, perhaps, but soccer was only introduced to the school in the late 1970s and their achievements since then have been commendable.

Two years ago, they sent three teams to an international soccer tournament in Leicester and two of those sides won the competitions in their age groups. Their other representatives only lost one game all week. When a Kilkenny boy does eventually sign for an English club, he'll most likely have gone to the same school as the hurling giants DJ Carey, Eddie Keher and Nicky Rackard.

There are other hurling strongholds where soccer is similarly thriving. There are 54 teams in the North Tipperary league now. There used to be around 12. The figures change from county to county, but the graph is always upward. In Roscommon, the number of schoolboy teams has risen from 18 to 98 in just six years. No coincidence, of course, that this particular dramatic upsurge dates almost exactly from the time when Sky Sports began to televise and give extensive coverage to the Premiership.

Indeed, almost as soon as the first ever soccer scouts landed in Roscommon in 1995, they discovered three players who they think might cut it at the highest level. Glasgow Celtic and Everton are the most interested parties in the county's youth, but the soccer brethren are hardly taken aback by the attention. Since the first ever primary schools soccer competition was introduced a couple of years ago to foster the game among the under-12s, they expect the number of visiting scouts to inevitably increase.

Elsewhere, in Connacht, Straid and Foxford, United won that province's senior league a couple of years ago. It was the first season that any team from Mayo had entered the competition. Meanwhile, Simon Webb, a boy who learned most of his soccer in Ballyhaunis, County Mayo, is currently in the Spurs youth team.

Galway has flirted with sending players to England for

much longer than its next-door neighbours. It's 20 years and more since Eamon Deacy went to Aston Villa and made it. Darragh Sheridan has followed the same path, while four other locals are billeted at various clubs, the most prominent of whom in the past season was, perhaps, Rory Ginty at Crystal Palace. In one of his first forays with the Palace first team, Ginty was brought on as a substitute for Attilio Lombardo.

Amid the end-of-season turmoil at Selhurst Park, Ginty was released by Palace, but another Irish teenager called Richie Kennedy is in the queue to take his place there. Kennedy hails from Rathgormack, a tiny village in the foothills of the Comeragh Mountains on the Waterford-Tipperary border. With a Gaelic football tradition pre-dating the foundation of the GAA, Rathgormack won back-to-back Waterford senior football titles in the mid-'90s. Organised soccer only arrived in the town around the same time as Jack Charlton became Irish manager, and Kennedy is the first offspring of the new relationship.

Charlton might claim a stake in Barry Conlon as well. Conlon is from Carrickmacross, the Monaghan town whose only prior link with international football is that Charlton, and his successor Mick McCarthy, often chose to base the Irish squad there. Conlon is now pursuing a professional career with Manchester City after spells at QPR and Plymouth Argyle. Monaghan and the bordering counties all paint the same picture as the rest of the country. The North-Eastern league which garners its players from Meath, Cavan, Monaghan, Louth and Westmeath has doubled its membership from 57 teams to 130 in the last five years.

The region has other boasts too. Drogheda pair, Gary Kelly and Ian Harte, and Dundalk's Steve Staunton are obvious enough candidates in this category, but the Wimbledon substitute goalkeeper is Brendan Murphy from Trim, who is also first choice with the Irish under-21s. Gary Tallon, a native of Lobinstown, plays up front for Mansfield Town having previously seen service with Blackburn Rovers and Kilmarnock. Navan's Johnathan Clarke is another one trying to make the breakthrough at Crystal Palace, and, as if to echo what's happening all over Ireland, none of these three towns has ever yielded professional footballers before.

Yet, just as in Kerry, the flourishing of one game in the various counties has not necessarily been at the expense of the other. Of course, there are still flashpoints in every town and village that houses goalposts of different dimensions, but they are less and less vehement and too many players have one foot in each camp for trouble to linger too long.

From his double life as manager of Bray Wanderers and scout for Newcastle United, Pat Devlin is better placed than most to explain the phenomenon which has seen towns all over rural Ireland become dots on the English soccer landscape. In recent years, he has spread his trawling for talent outside the traditional urban areas and into the countryside.

'I think the Jack Charlton era left a huge impression regarding soccer in this country. It made a huge impression, especially on all the young kids and families around the place and it's a terrible, sad thing that within that era, we didn't capitalise on it. The structures required were never put in place because I think everybody just concentrated on the good team we had and didn't care about anything else.

'It was an awful lack of foresight, and to be honest, the reason players are coming through in the numbers that they are now is just because soccer became very, very popular. It's not because we have enough coaches with the required expertise in Kerry or Wexford or wherever, we just have people who are genuinely interested in the game, who will go out of their way and volunteer for the love of the game. I think that the real credit has to go to the people who run all the teams, who don't really gain anything out of it.

'Not the people who make it to the top in the FAI but the guy who had this ambition to win the local cup, and started his team, and whatever. Without them, we wouldn't have the players. I think too that a lot of the players have purely natural talent, and we jump on the bandwagon and say a lot of people have done very well by the kids. For a lot of these kids, it's just natural ability developed a bit by the local team manager. A lot of credit should be going to these people but if it was more structured, this conveyor belt that we have would be even fuller.'

With this in mind, Devlin is orchestrating an innovative scheme involving Adidas, Newcastle United and his own club, Bray Wanderers. Every Monday night during the 1997/98 season, he ran coaching schools in three different centres in south Dublin and Wicklow involving 26 coaches and 400 kids. There are plans to expand the operation to include centres in Malahide, Athlone and Sligo. The aim is for the kids between the ages of 12 and 15 to receive the best coaching available, and Devlin insists there is no pressure on the most talented players to commit themselves to one of his clubs.

'I don't want nothing off these people. If you don't want to go to Newcastle at the end of this, you're still not going to go. But at least we'll have educated you properly in the basics of the game and I'm convinced that initiatives like this one are the way forward for Irish soccer.'

Newcastle are not the only English club to be aware of the rich pickings over here. One of Liam Brady's first initiatives upon being appointed Director of Youth Development at Arsenal was to establish a link between Highbury and the Dublin and District Schoolboys' League, where Arsenal sponsor the DDSL Under-13 team. As part of the deal, the Dublin players are coached up to eight times a season by the club's coaches, and the full squad travel to London once a year to play their Arsenal contemporaries. Tranmere Rovers, meanwhile, have exploited John Aldridge's connections with this country to set up a nursery type arrangement with Stella Maris.

All the time, competition to grab the most gifted Irish youngsters is intensifying. After a Blackpool official mentioned in a Dublin newspaper that his club were on the look-out for an Irish scout, they received 40 or so applications for the job. Recognising the prevailing trends in Irish soccer, the club decided they needed a couple of country-based scouts as well as somebody in Dublin. They know that the best players may no longer be in the most obvious places.

In America in the early '90s, an economist worked out that the average basketball-playing, black teenager had more chance of being hit by lightning than fulfilling his dream of making it as a professional in the National Basketball Association (NBA). If the statistical probability for an Irish youngster vis à vis the Premiership cannot be that different, this doesn't stop them dreaming in their thousands.

But visiting the home of Michael Foley, a talented 14-year-old Dubliner last January, it was instructive to discover that while the boy himself was already verbally committed to Liverpool, his younger brother and five other neighbouring children were being actively courted by English clubs. This nondescript street in the newish, working-class suburb of Hartstown, west Dublin, with maybe 20 houses on it, had seven kids nurturing fantasies of making it in England.

What chance all of them making it? What chance none? And how many of their country's cousins will be there with them? Therein lies the rub.

Chapter One

Royzone

'Cork is no place for sensitive folk. To succeed you have to have the skin of a rhinoceros, the dissimulation of a crocodile, the quality of a hare, the speed of a hawk. Otherwise, the word for every Corkman is to get out and get out quick.'
SEAN O'FAOLAIN

Roy Keane is the dream. His is the honour and the glory, the car, the house and the boot deal. He is what every young Irish boy who plays the game aspires to becoming. The highest-paid Irish footballer ever, captain of Manchester United, the most successful English club of the decade, and central to his country's hopes of qualifying for any major tournament in the near future. On match days, the vendors around Old Trafford sell Irish tricolours with Keane's face printed on the white portion just like once they flogged the French tricolour with the image of Eric Cantona. The weekend after he incurred the injury that put him out for most of the 1997/98 season, more than one chorus of 'Keano' rang around Old Trafford to commemorate his absence. Midway through his professional career, this is the kind of adulation he inspires.

But that is only the half of it. Keane is the only Irish player of the modern era to be comprehensively booed at Lansdowne Road, and he divides followers of the game in this country like nobody else. The September day against Leeds United that he clumsily fouled Alf Inge Haaland, and tore his cruciate ligament in the process, there were people in Ireland actually laughing about it, saying it was no more than he deserved. The damage may have been self-inflicted but it was difficult to imagine England supporters reacting in the same way towards Alan Shearer's injury when qualification for a World Cup was still in the balance.

The irony of it all is that up to that point, Keane was actually voted Ireland's player of the year for his performances in a green shirt and as Mick McCarthy's team were subsequently edged out in a World Cup play-off with Belgium, it is not an exaggeration to say that his presence over the two legs might have tipped the advantage the other way. Envy, though, is the most negative of all emotions, and for the same reason that Roy Keane is the dream for nascent footballers all over the country, he is begrudged each element of his success by others.

There are many theories as to why. His abrasive playing style and the fact that he plays for Manchester United definitely have something to do with it, as does the fact that he has been perceived as being less than committed to the Ireland jersey. His refusal to play the media game off the field is important too. Those Irish players who readily give out their home numbers to reporters inevitably get a much easier ride from the newspapers than those who don't, and no Irish international has ever got quite as rough a ride from the tabloids as Keane.

There is something intrinsically sad about all this because Keane's story has more than the whiff of a fairytale about it and deserves to be celebrated more than it is. Small for his age, and struggling for proper recognition throughout his adolescence, the runt of the litter eventually rose to become top dog. Against the odds, he was picked up by an English club at an age when most scouts had already given up on his generation, and moved on to their younger brothers; then after only a couple of months he was catapulted into the first team at Forest – Brian Clough's last great hunch and his legacy to the English game.

But nobody ever prepared Keane for the vagaries of fame the way they instructed him in the arts of the game, and consequently, he has often found it difficult to handle. If some of the mistakes he has made off the field have been worse than others, all have suffered tabloid magnification. The great pity is that they detract from what he has achieved on the field. To teenage boys with notions of making it in the professional game, Keane's career is a living, breathing lesson about the attitude required to do so.

Here is a man, who, even after he signed for Manchester United – a move which brought him perilously near the summit of personal achievement – was still conscious enough of the need to improve, to come back in the afternoons and work on his touch. He is a monument to the virtues of dedication and determination, and every youngster of impressionable age should be told: 'With a little bit of luck, and an incredible work ethic, all this can be yours too.'

The boy who is now paid £20,000 per week by Manchester United was born in Cork on 10 August 1971, and grew up in two different local authority houses in Mayfield, a country village long since absorbed into the urban sprawl of Cork's northside. During Keane's formative years, his was a city smote by the closure of Ford cars and Dunlop Rubber, two of the region's biggest employers. The Keanes knew the spectre of unemployment well, but Roy's childhood was still 'very happy' and his family were offended when some journalists began dubbing him 'the boy from the ghetto made good'. Upset at this depiction, his mother Marie told one interviewer that they were 'ordinary working class people', just like the majority of Keane's peers in the professional game.

'People ask me where I'm from when I'm in England, and I always say Cork first, then Ireland,' says Keane. 'It's Cork first and Ireland second. I'm very proud of where I'm from, proud to be from Mayfield and Cork. I had a very happy childhood and I love coming back. I don't get back with United as often as I did with Forest though, and the thing is that I don't even like coming back for a couple of days, I like to come back for a couple of weeks when I can.'

The landmarks of his childhood are still extant. The number 8 bus still spans the city from Bishopstown to Mayfield, stopping outside the Cotton Ball. The community school and GAA club, which both recognised in him a useful, if diminutive corner-forward, continue to thrive, as does Brian Dillon's boxing club where he had a brief fistic flirtation that English newspapers like to dwell on in their profiles. The heart of Blackpool is still the yellow, green and black of the Glen Hall. The property of Glen Rovers still stands, where some bright sparks in Rockmount FC used to take advantage of its status in the community by commandeering its location as a meeting place for their younger teams.

Rockmount wasn't his local club but it was his birthright. His mother's brothers, Mick and Pat Lynch, played on and managed their teams, and Roy's own elder siblings, Denis and Johnson, wore the green and yellow strip before him. When he reached a certain age, it was natural for him to be brought along too. 'All I remember about it now is that it was a fair trek from our house down to Blackpool for a nine-year-old.'

His first managers christened him 'boiler man' – the fellow they looked to if they needed to get things going in midfield. Nine years old, playing in a team that was Under-11, they voted him player of the year at the end of his first season. Sinking back into his couch, Timmy Murphy, one of the side's managers, remembers a time when his own beard was more pepper than salt, and Roy Keane was his boiler man.

'Football mad, he was. Rain, hail or snow, that's all that interested him. He was always first down for training,' says Murphy. 'At that time, we used to train in the Old Christians' rugby pitch because it was too far to go out the seven miles to Rockmount Park. We'd sneak in before any of the rugby crowd would see us and train away.'

Mention Murphy, and Keane will immediately append the

name of the late Gene O'Sullivan to the anecdote. Murphy and O'Sullivan were the double act behind the Rockmount team where Keane spent nine years cutting his football teeth. In the days when it appeared that English football would never recognise his gifts, it was Murphy and O'Sullivan who consoled Keane and assured him that his determination would not go untapped. They could do so with some confidence.

The little bantam in their charge may have been small for his age, but they had heard about him hanging a football from a clothes line out the back of his house so he could practise his heading; they had seen him get a holiday job in an off-licence that required him to lift cases of beer upstairs in the hope that it would strengthen his legs, and somehow they knew. They filled his head with talk of how the bigger fell harder and watched him grow to the task.

In the great fable that is Keane's life, Timmy Murphy and Gene O'Sullivan play a truly heroic part; ordinary, decent football men, coaching a team for the love of the game, and in the half-hope that one of their number might some day make it big. They embody the sort of people who are the lifeblood of the schoolboy game. There are thousands more just like them all over the country: buffing and polishing teenage talent, using ingenuity and enthusiasm to overcome deficient resources and fostering dreams of glory. Many will remain unsung heroes, their names never writ large via the exploits of a former player, but Murphy and O'Sullivan will always be remembered for nurturing a schoolboy team of all the talents, and the midfielder of a generation.

In a city riven by intense football rivalry, few would dispute the claim that the Rockmount team that Keane played with was the best schoolboy outfit that Cork has ever produced. They won six consecutive league and cup doubles, five of them played international football at some level, and the same quintet formed the spine of the Cork team which won the Kennedy Cup in 1986. Their most famous graduate is always anxious to pay homage to the club's part in his rise.

'People always refer to me as coming from Cobh

Ramblers, but I was only with Cobh for a season. I'd spent nine great years at Rockmount. We had a great team, we had so much success in Cork, and the only thing that we never won was a national title. We had great players, Clarkey (Derek Clarke) in goal, Paul McCarthy, Damien Martin, Len Downey, Alan O'Sullivan, we had so many.'

So many indeed that in the beginning, Keane wasn't even their most glittering prize. That honour fell to Alan O'Sullivan, a mercurial left winger who would spend four-and-a-half ill-starred years at Luton Town before returning to Cork and the relative anonymity of local football. Paul McCarthy, a strapping centre-half who averaged 20 goals a season before signing for Brighton and Hove Albion at age 16, was another with a burgeoning reputation. Almost the entire team went cross-channel for trials at some point but, of the rest, only McCarthy has endured to play 300 odd games in the lower divisions with Brighton and Wycombe Wanderers.

Although he was deemed good enough to captain the Kennedy Cup team, Keane's lack of inches often told against him. After one Irish Under-15 trial, the manager told him that he wouldn't be required again because he was just too small. The disappointment enveloped him as he slumped into the back seat and was driven the 160 miles home to Cork. Lesser boys would have had their spirits broken by such incidents; Keane only became fired up by them.

Neither could myopic scouts see the scope for physical development. Brighton were once persuaded by Paul McCarthy's father to take Keane on trial but retracted the offer at the last moment. Their Irish scout told the manager that Keane was too small, had a dodgy temperament and that they really shouldn't bother. The same month that Brighton lost the Goldstone Ground, and narrowly avoided relegation to the non-leagues, Keane was winning his third Premiership title in four seasons with Manchester United.

In professional circumstance, Len Downey was always the closest on the Rockmount team to Roy Keane. A tall and talented centre-forward, Downey also possessed the unhappy knack of being consistently overlooked by the English scouts. Whereas Keane's lack was principally physical, Downey's appeared mental. His tendency to lose concentration was such that some at Rockmount always reckoned he played better if he got a wake-up belt early on in games.

By the age of 17, the pair were still in Cork while many of their contemporaries were already on apprenticeships in England. They thought their chance had passed, and the only consolation prize available was a League of Ireland contract. Cork City courted both players but only succeeded in signing Downey. Keane had a prior agreement with Cobh Ramblers and, as they were quickest to register him, he became their player.

City and Ramblers were offering the young hopefuls identical terms: a shot at the League of Ireland, a few bob while they were trying, and a place on the inaugural FAI/FAS soccer apprenticeship course in Dublin. It wasn't quite the dream but it was something. Keane had left school at 15, and two years down the line, this was about the best job offer he could have hoped for.

Keane's attitude towards the course now is instructive. He didn't like living in Dublin, hated the travelling up and down, but loved the regime. 'I enjoyed the training all right, and especially playing a match every day. But I missed my family. I never really liked being in Dublin, it was my first time living away from home, and I didn't enjoy it. We were getting the train up every Monday morning at half past seven, and coming down every Friday night to play matches at weekends. I didn't like it, but it definitely improved me.'

According to Downey, their enthusiasm for the half past seven train waned as the season wore on. They'd often aim for the nine o'clock before finally settling for the 11, and some weeks they'd wangle it so they didn't have to go back until Tuesday. But when they did manage to get there, Keane never stinted with the work. He had only begun to realise the difference that full-time training could make to his game, and over the course of that year, he began a filling-out process that probably only ended when he reached Manchester United.

'The one thing about Roy on that course was the way that he trained,' says Richie Parsons, a fellow trainee who now plays in the League of Ireland for Bray Wanderers. 'He gave everything at every drill, whether it was taking shots or passing, you name it, he constantly tried to get better all the time. When we were doing laps of the field, it wouldn't be unusual for Roy to go 150 yards or so ahead of the rest of us, and stay there. His attitude was unbelievable.' Determined and dedicated as ever.

Cobh Ramblers were quick to integrate Keane into their first team, and entering a dressing-room where local legends, Alex Ludzic and Mick 'Slap' O'Keefe, held court, he kept his counsel for the most part. He knew he was good enough to be there but he also knew his place. Ask Cobh's then manager, Liam McMahon, what Keane was like in the team dressing-room, and he laughs: 'I don't think that I ever heard him speak out loud.'

Keane's reticence didn't evaporate once he crossed the white lines either, and he was far from the dominant, vocal figure he would later become. Nevertheless, he soon became so central to Ramblers' plans that McMahon would go to extraordinary lengths to have him in his team. One Saturday afternoon, this necessitated a car waiting outside St Colman's Park for Keane to finish playing an FAI youths cup match against Belvedere before ferrying him to Donegal for a League of Ireland tie the following day. Eight hours after the final whistle in Cobh, the car pulled into Jackson's Hotel, Ballybofey. A lot to ask of an 18-year-old boy, perhaps. Keane was only ever going to give them one answer.

Nobody remembers much about the Finn Harps game now, but the youths' cup match has passed into folklore. Belvedere snatched a last-minute equaliser to force a replay in Dublin. The game was fixed for 18 February 1990, and among the spectators was a man called Noel McCabe; history would later remember him as the scout who discovered Roy Keane for Nottingham Forest.

This was Keane's lucky break, and without it, all that diligence, all that marvellous application might well have come to naught. What if Belvedere hadn't equalised and there had been no replay? What if McCabe had decided to attend another game instead, and spotted some other bright young thing? What if, as he was entitled to do under his contract, Keane had chosen not to play for the youths team that weekend? What if? indeed.

These days, McCabe scouts for Liverpool, his stock in the business forever favourably linked to his one great find. Where others had dithered about temperament and size, McCabe saw only latent talent. Belvedere trounced Cobh 4-0 but even in a losing team, Keane caught his eye. Sitting down in his Donnycarney home that evening to write his report, McCabe finished on the emphatic note: 'He is, in my opinion, a player to go on trial to Forest right away.'

When Cobh's chairman, John O'Rourke, sidled up to Keane after the game to appraise him of an earlier conversation he'd had with McCabe, the player was unmoved. 'I'd heard that kind of thing hundreds of times before. There's a scout watching you today, and if you do well, there could be a trial in it for you. I didn't take much notice when I heard it because I didn't want to be disappointed again.'

Three days later, Keane and McCabe were sitting down for tea in the Ashling Hotel near Heuston Station, working out the logistics of a trip to the City Ground. McCabe has had the same conversation with close on a hundred different teenagers but none gave off as good a first impression as this one. 'The boy wanted to be a footballer so bad,' says McCabe. 'He was so eager and enthusiastic that when I left the meeting, I felt that here was a boy who would swim across to England if I asked him to.'

The day that they accompanied Keane to the City Ground to negotiate his transfer, John O'Rourke and John Meade, Cobh's chairman and secretary respectively, got a similar vibe. In the car journey up from Heathrow, he had the manic air of a person who was ready to sign anything the club put in front of him. It's an account of the event he doesn't dispute. 'I was desperate. I was thinking: "Well, I'm 18 now, if Forest don't take me, this is probably going to be it." '

For releasing him, Cobh received a total of £47,000. It was

a reasonable enough return for an unproven youngster, but one they could have added an extra zero to if they had procured a sell-on clause. Their failure to do so has drawn criticism from many down the years. 'Nobody in Ireland ever had a £3.75m player before,' says McMahon. 'We sold Roy as raw potential and despite what they might say now, nobody could have seen him making it so big so soon.'

Cobh's lack of foresight has been a lesson to National League clubs, all of whom push hard for sell-on clauses now. Another offshoot of Keane's inexorable rise to fame was similar to that which occurs when a pop band from a certain city makes it big. Pretty soon, that city will be swamped by record company representatives trawling for similar acts, and Keane's dramatic ascent into the Forest first team inspired just such an indecent flurry among English football clubs, many of whom had always scouted over here anyway.

Liam Tuohy remembers old contacts of his in England ringing up: 'They were asking me did I have any more like Roy Keane over here. You'd swear that there was a Roy Keane standing on every corner waiting to be picked up. In all the fuss they forgot that Keane was playing in the League of Ireland at 17. Not many young fellas manage that, so it wasn't as if he was unknown or that he'd suddenly come out of nowhere.'

His first pre-season trip was to Haarlem in Holland, a glamorous assignment for somebody whose childhood summer holidays stretched as far as his uncle's caravan in Garretstown and a one-off trip to Butlins. On the way to the final of the youths' tournament that Forest were playing in, Keane lined out at right full-back, right-wing, centre-half and midfield, each time confounding the club's chief scout, Alan Hill, a little bit more. 'He'd been brilliant all through but against Barcelona in the final, he was absolutely outstanding,' says Hill. 'I knew after that game that this lad had a big future in the game.'

Hill's gushing progress report to Brian Clough about his latest protégé intrigued the Forest manager, who soon turned up at a reserve team game to see for himself. On discovering that Keane was only a substitute, Clough waited until half-time before sidling up to the dug-out, and telling the reserves' manager, Archie Gemmill, to replace his son Scott with 'the Irishman'. Gemmill ignored the request until, with 20 minutes to go, Clough vaulted the hoardings and ordered him: 'Get your son off and put the Irishman on.'

Keane's brief cameo wasn't as impressive as Hill had hoped, but Clough was still smitten. 'Brian was such a genius at spotting youngsters,' says Hill. 'He could always spot something that the rest of us couldn't. I think he saw Roy make a couple of forward runs and then stick somebody on their backside and that was enough. Afterwards, he told me: "The kid has everything, you just have to encourage him".'

Delighted with having broken into the reserve team so early, Keane tagged along as the rest of the side went out for a few drinks after the game. When he turned up for training the next morning, his world started to spin at a faster pace. With Steve Hodge a late injury doubt, there was a place going in the first team squad for a game at Liverpool. Clough had a choice between Phil Starbuck and Keane, and with one swift and arbitrary decision, the course of a life was changed irrevocably.

In the dressing-room at Anfield, Keane was busying himself helping Liam O'Kane to lay out the kit before Clough pulled him aside and said: 'Irishman, put the number seven shirt on, you're playing.' The years have blurred his vision of that night but one incident that evening has stayed with him. 'At one stage, I was running back and Steve McMahon was running next to me. I remember looking at him and thinking: "this is it."'

After an excellent début at Anfield, some games were easier to cope with than others. The day that Spurs came to the City ground, Keane had to listen to a stream of verbal abuse from Paul Gascoigne. In the players' lounge after the game, he told a local journalist how horrified he'd been by the constant barrage. On Monday afternoon, it was the back page lead in the *Nottingham Evening Post*. By Tuesday morning, it was 'Keane slams foul-mouth Gazza' in every English tabloid.

Keane had just learned his first lesson about talking to the press, the hard way. In time, there would be many more such lessons as he began to earn a degree of notoriety via the favoured path of errant footballers: late night incidents. Whether it was being ejected from a Nottingham wine bar or becoming involved in a fracas on a pre-season tour of the Channel Islands, Keane began to earn a reputation that he's never quite shaken off, even though some attacks have been completely unjustified. In one instance, a Cork woman, a former neighbour, sued him for slander following an exchange outside a nightclub. She alleged that he called her a whore. He said he didn't. After an attendant media circus, the judge ruled in his favour.

Keane was slow to realise that his new-found fame also had a downside. Any story with him at its centre was now big news, and that turning the other cheek wasn't his preferred method of dealing with abuse didn't help his cause any. 'If somebody has a go at me, then I'll have a go back. That's just the way I am. People always ask me if I've settled down, and I'm afraid to say "yes" because as soon as I say that, I go off a week later and do something stupid.'

If the Gascoigne incident gave Keane a glimpse of the new reality he was facing, the rest of his début season was more a dream than a nightmare. Three months after the Liverpool game, Forest handed him the keys to a brand new Ford Orion. His first club car, his first ever car, he'd been so unprepared for its arrival that he hadn't even learned how to drive. Before Christmas, Clough gave him an improved contract and as he left the manager's office, he sensed for the first time that, even though he was still togging out in the reserves' dressing-room, he was going to be in the first team for a long time. That first year, he shared a house with Gary Bowyer, son of former Forest great Ian, and life was good.

'For the first time, I was making a few bob for myself, and it was so exciting being in the first team that I never really had any time to be homesick or anything. My plan had been to spend a couple of years in the reserves before making the breakthrough.'

The Manchester United scout, Les Kershaw, was sitting in the stand that fateful evening at Anfield. He reported back to Alex Ferguson that Forest gave a début to a young Irish player who looked promising. A couple of months later, Ferguson got his first close-up view. 'They came to Old Trafford to play us, and when the ball was kicked off, it went back to Robbo [Bryan Robson],' says Ferguson. 'Keane comes flying through and absolutely cemented him. I'm sitting there, thinking: "That's a bit cheeky, coming here and tackling like that." '

Soon after that, the United manager read in a newspaper that Keane had once written to every club in England seeking a trial. Enraged at this perceived oversight, Ferguson took the article to his scouting office and demanded that somebody find Keane's missive to United. Fortunately for the employees concerned, Keane eventually told another journalist that United was the only club he hadn't written to. In the midst of his teenage desperation to be given the chance to play in England, he'd decided that he probably wasn't good enough for United so it wasn't worth wasting the stamp.

Ferguson kept tabs on Keane all through his début season, and a couple of weeks after United had won the European Cup Winners' Cup, he nearly got his man in a swap deal that would have seen Neil Webb go the other way. But Clough was too canny to give Keane up cheaply, and two years later Ferguson paid £3.75m to get his man. Shortly before completing the transfer, Ferguson rang Jack Charlton for an opinion. The then Irish manager was characteristically blunt. 'I just told him to get 'im bought,' says Charlton. 'I told him he'd be able to sell him on to Europe for 6 or 7 million in a couple of years.'

The dynamic behind the signing of Keane tells us much about his value system. Having first agreed lucrative terms with Blackburn Rovers, Keane went to talk to Alex Ferguson. Over a game of snooker and some lunch at Ferguson's house, they sussed each other out. Both say the conversation was almost exclusively about football with money only coming in after Keane had decided Old Trafford was definitely where he wanted to go. Keane eventually signed for significantly less wages than he was being offered by Blackburn Rovers, claiming the opportunity to win trophies was more important than expanding an already sizable pay packet. Alan Shearer made exactly the opposite decision, and has paid for it dearly in terms of club honours.

At the time Keane joined United, he was the most coveted player in England. He wasn't however what he is now – the best midfielder in the Premiership. Even a cursory glance at old photographs points up one startling difference. The slight figure with ample space in the red jersey of Nottingham Forest now fills out every one of the various United strips, and this physical development is matched by his growth as a player. After some teething troubles, he settled in to become the mainstay of the United midfield, usurping the position and status of first Bryan Robson and then Paul Ince. Ironically, there are elements of both of them about Keane's game: he has Robson's colossal ability to swing important matches like cup finals and Ince's irritating capacity for chronic dissent and the odd rash lunge.

While the rest of the football world raved about Ince during United's romp to their 1994 Double, Alex Ferguson and Brian Kidd were privately discussing how Keane had overtaken him in their estimation. Said Ferguson: 'We felt at that stage that Roy was going to become a better player for us than Ince.' Twelve months later, Ince, once spoken of as a future United captain, was off-loaded to Inter Milan, and Ferguson began negotiations to extend and vastly improve Keane's contract. Having never been shy of extolling Keane's virtues, the manager was prepared to put his money where his mouth was and he certainly needed to.

In the summer of 1996, Barcelona had come looking for Keane. Conscious of the fact that his first initial United contract expired the following year, they were eager for him to take advantage of the Bosman ruling. The offer was simple: £3 million to sign on, and an annual wage of half that thereafter. The extras were the usual stuff of continental tenders, a luxury villa here, the club president's private jet at his disposal there. Keane considered the offer, and at least two more of similar lustre from Italy, and then he signed a new four-year contract with United.

Ferguson made Keane the highest paid player at Old Trafford on £20,000 a week, and the player is said to have had a clause inserted in his contract which entitles him to a pay rise to match the wage of any new signing. Perhaps a more impressive little detail than the wage figures themselves, however, is the fact that Keane had turned down more money to leave than he accepted to stay, and much like the circumstances in which he had initially signed, the United fans loved him all the more for it. Loyalty is obviously its own reward.

As his love affair with the Old Trafford supporters continued to blossom, his relationship with Ireland's supporters had deteriorated so much by the autumn of 1996 that during the first ten minutes of a World Cup qualifier against Iceland at Lansdowne Road, he was roundly booed by a section of the crowd. In true, stubborn Keane style, he ignored the taunts to deliver a consummate performance at centre-half and to win the man-of-the-match award.

The supporters' anger emanated from the fact that he had missed 18 international matches out of the previous 22, and, deprived of Keane for crucial fixtures, Ireland had failed to qualify for Euro '96. On two occasions, he was absent for an international match on a Wednesday before lining out for United at the weekend. In his defence, Keane would tell people the injuries were always genuine, and the two hasty re-appearances could be explained by medicine, a few days being a long time in the world of groin strains.

Given his dreadful luck with injuries, and the amount of club games he was missing, the fans might have accepted this if the US Cup debacle hadn't made Keane public enemy number one. His decision not to travel to what was essentially a second-rate competition should not have been a problem, but it became an unseemly episode which exposed the player's naïvité when it comes to matters of course.

He absented himself from the games without ever

contacting the team manager Mick McCarthy; there were vague claims about phone calls to the FAI offices; there was even a bogus Roy Keane phoning the team hotel. Worst of all, there was a statement to the Press Association which McCarthy first heard of through reporters. Afterwards, Keane was suitably contrite about the entire mess, but in many ways, the US Cup was the worst of his career in microcosm. He made a silly mistake which the tabloids latched on to with gusto and aggrandized. For weeks, they had reporters keeping vigil outside his parents' house in Cork, and regularly ran invasive photographs of him getting a pram ready for his youngest daughter or putting his two-year-old into the car.

In all the brouhaha, there were several unenlightened statements made about Keane's international career, with 'He's never done it for Ireland' being the most common and ignorant of them all. As far back as Seville in 1992, Keane so dominated a game against Spain that Diego Maradona described him as the best young midfielder in Europe. Two years later, he was voted Ireland's player of the US World Cup by RTE's viewers.

The Templeacre Tavern is perched high on a hill overlooking Cork city from the north side. It's a nondescript pub, save for walls which are covered in photographs of successful Temple United teams that have been backboned by Roy Keane's brothers. There is no Jimmy Five Bellies figure in Keane's life, just a tight circle of family and friends back in Cork to whom he retreats now and again, although possibly not as often as he would like. The Templeacre is where he goes when he's with them, and its denizens have never broken his trust.

Once, when Radio Ireland rang looking for somebody in the bar to talk about their most celebrated customer's elevation to the Manchester United captaincy, the staff waited for Keane's permission before taking the call. On the day in 1993 when United paid a then British transfer record for his signature, journalists were trawling two countries in search of him. He was in fact sitting in the Templeacre, flanked by his brothers. And in the midst of the US Cup controversy, when the tabloids were in a Keane-stalking frenzy, the barstaff made fools of the various newshounds who came sniffing around, and enjoyed doing so.

In the Templeacre, they'll vouchsafe that Keane hasn't forgotten where he came from, and it's easy to take them at their word. It's a couple of years now since he moved his parents to a detached house five miles outside the city, and local legend has it that each of his brothers and sister have been bought a house of their own too. The city is regularly awash with rumours about Keane's latest 'purchase' and he has been linked with nightclubs, pubs and even the local football club.

But Cork is like that, and the co-relation between his birthplace and his personality should never be underestimated. Nor should his love of the place. Both of his daughters have been brought back to Cork to be christened, and when he married Theresa Doyle, a Nottingham native and mother of his two kids, it was in his local church. A small, private ceremony, attended only by immediate family, it made the front pages of national newspapers, tabloid and broadsheet.

It is said that jerseys signed by the entire Manchester United team are available to worthy causes in the city on request and financial donations are not unheard of either. At least one charitable institution on Cork's northside had a new roof installed thanks to an anonymous benefactor reckoned to be Keane. This is one more side to this complex individual. Just as it's hard to reconcile the snarling midfielder who stamped on Gareth Southgate in an emotionally-charged FA Cup semi-final with the image of him stopping on his way into a hotel to hand one of his Ireland World Cup jerseys to a child in a wheelchair, so too is it difficult to imagine the media-shy footballer as mystery benefactor.

For somebody who grew up without much to spare, money is certainly important to Keane – but his devotion to Manchester United shows that it has never been the be-all and end-all. Early on in his fame, he did drive a fire-engine-red Mercedes with the number plate Roy 1, and he was castigated for the vanity of it. Yet older and supposedly wiser players than Keane boast personalised number plates well into their thirties. It's a gauche trapping of fame that wealthy footballers routinely award themselves, and as much a part of the stereotype as the mock tudor mansion. Keane was all of 22 when he got rid of his.

He still has plenty of the accoutrements of the successful young athlete. A six-figure boot deal with Diadora, a mobile phone endorsement with Motorola, and a £500,000 house in Cheshire. He could have much more but his solicitor, Michael Kennedy, will tell you that he turns down 95 per cent of his commercial opportunities off the pitch, preferring quality of life to the accumulation of further wealth. Schmoozing with the sponsors has never quite been his thing.

It was the Wimbledon manager Joe Kinnear who first described Keane as 'the heartbeat of the United team' and the metaphor is wholly appropriate. In the big games, his outsize determination drives the others on, and in the canters, he just keeps everything ticking over. At this point in his career, Keane's sometime reluctance to use his left foot, his cantankerous temperament and the fact that he doesn't score as many goals as he should, are the sum of his flaws, and they are just minor quibbles next to what he brings to the United team.

Way back when he was first injured, around the time that Manchester United were in particularly scintillating form, thrashing the likes of Sheffield Wednesday and Barnsley, the assistant manager Brian Kidd punctured a few of the balloons that were going up by pointing out that, come March and April, the team would feel the loss of Keane most. Kidd is rarely wrong, and sure enough, when Manchester United tumbled out of the Champions' League to Monaco, and let Arsenal overtake them in the Premiership, Keane was the name on everybody's lips. In his own end of season analysis, Alex Ferguson lamented the loss of Keane by saying: 'There would have been a few angry half-time dressing-rooms if he was playing.'

Shortly after that injury occurred, Keane took a phone call from Paul McGrath. The two are near neighbours, and their wives Theresa and Caroline are good friends. In the guise of the gnarled old pro whose knees are the stuff of medical legend, McGrath was ringing up to offer advice about how Keane should watch what he drank during the rehabilitation. Keane's response was to laugh about who the advice was coming from, but in his application to his recuperation, there was to be no joking. It is not unusual for footballers to put on two stone while recovering from a major knee operation. At one stage, Keane had lost the same amount of poundage through sheer physical work.

As the English season petered out, word reached the newspapers that Keane had forsaken his summer holiday to spend lonely mornings at United's training ground, The Cliff. Injury robbing Keane of the United captaincy just a month after it had been given to him hurt him a lot, and he was anxious to continue working on his fitness for the forthcoming campaign. The boy who once hung a football from his clothes line to practise his heading has made good, and the words 'dedication' and 'determination' spring to mind once more.

'The truth is that modesty does not suit Cork people.
There is a certain swagger in their walk, known locally
as a gaatch, a certain bravado in their speech which
even in times of adversity never quite deserts them.'
TOM MCELLIGOT.

Chapter Two

Down among the agate type

Nobody in Ireland ever dreams of playing for Forfar Athletic. In those moments of childhood reverie, when little boys imagine themselves scoring the winner in an FA Cup final at Wembley, it is invariably in the red of Manchester United or Liverpool, not the dark blue of Halifax Town. From the first time football intrudes upon a teenager's life with such seriousness that he dares to think that one day he might make it to The Show, he never gives a thought to the prospect of togging out before a few hundred people in some ramshackle venue or other.

In the pursuit of the dream it is all or nothing, because for every prospect who leaves Ireland for Britain, the sacrifice to be made is huge. That the vast majority of those who fail to make the grade return home from Premiership or Division One clubs rather than drop down a division or three to play first team football only confirms this much. When you have so often visualised yourself on the biggest stages, it seems, the reality of life in the minor leagues can be too difficult to contemplate.

Some, however, can't let go that easily once they get on the merry-go-round, they find it hard to step off and end up living their lives among the agate type of the sports results pages. In between the tiny print, somewhere along the margins of white space, there are Irishmen playing out the less than full hand that sporting destiny has dealt them.

This is the story of two such men who have adapted quite happily to life on the fringe.

One has represented his country, the other hasn't, yet they share a common dignity of purpose. Their love of the game takes precedence above all else. For Kieran O'Regan and John Donegan, this has long since ceased to be about money, though some of it wouldn't go astray. They never made it to the duvet covers or the pull-out posters stage. Their faces will never adorn the cover of any magazine and their life stories will never be serialised in the tabloids. When a reporter from home phones them up, it's a novelty not a nuisance.

But they too were prospects once. Kieran O'Regan represented Ireland at nearly all levels and John Donegan had more than one top English club chasing his signature at 19. Their aspirations of making it at the highest level were grounded in reality, not just fanciful notions. Anybody who played with either of them growing up will tell you that in their own towns they were the best footballers of their generation.

They chased their dreams then, but settled for something less: for never seeing themselves on Sky Sports, for never banking a £20,000 cheque at the end of a week, for always struggling, like the rest of us, in the elusive search for financial security. Despite all this, the game still grips them. They do not consider themselves failures. Why should anybody else?

Maybe 50 yards from Halifax's main shopping area, a sign directs you to go right at the Wallis Simpson Hotel before Eureka, the primary-coloured Children's Museum that is one of the town's main tourist attractions. Half a mile on, the road dips, and between the cover of some overhanging trees, it's just possible to make out the four floodlight pylons of the local football ground. To the side, halfway up a street called Hunger Hill, there's a lane that affords a brief glimpse into the history of Halifax Town.

The disused turnstiles are smattered with the detritus of a thousand match days, choked by the undergrowth blossoming in their midst and rusting all the while. Above them, there's a sign that reads 'Adults £1, Children 50p'. These down-at-heel metal structures are a suitable metaphor for a club that has seen better days. Once upon a time, 36,885 people filed through here to see the home team take on Spurs in the FA Cup. The prices listed are a throwback to that bygone era, when Halifax Town were in the Football League proper, and these turnstiles were oiled by the constant whirr of traffic.

Now, Halifax play in the GM Vauxhall Conference and everything is different. The Conference is English football's underworld, a place where thirty-something professionals often go to cushion the transition back to the real world with a part-time contract. There they meet kids who dream of going all the way, and others who've never been. If their ground is up to standard, the team who wins the Conference gain promotion to Nationwide Division Three. In August 1997, the bookmakers rated Halifax as 66-1 outsiders to manage this feat.

Over at the main entrance, the billboard that distracts passing motorists is weather-beaten and desperate for a coat of paint. Garish yellow flyers are posted one on top of the other, and the very latest announces the impending arrival of Ossett Town, representatives of the Northern Counties East League, for the FA Cup third qualifying round. Not the sort of glamorous FA Cup tie that non-league clubs usually dream about.

On weekday mornings, this ground has been known to echo to the sounds of Frank Sinatra, the groundsman feeling that a suitable soundtrack allows him do his work that bit better. But at lunchtime on this particular Wednesday, the reception area is empty. Loitering around there, the first thing to catch your eye is the sign above the door which reads: 'This is The Shay'. It hardly inspires fear when on the wall to the right, there's a photograph of the last Halifax team who tumbled out of the Football League in 1993, one more sorry reminder of how far they've fallen.

Down the tunnel, the remains of what used to be a speedway track insulates the crowd from the pitch. The main stand is an assortment of old, wooden seats, some in need of replacing, more already gone. At one end, this edifice is bookended by a small blue prefabricated building. Unimpressive? Yes. Run down? Definitely. The nerve centre of a football club plotting their return to the big time? Unlikely, but true.

Here, among the discarded footballs and corner-flag stumps, the management duo of Halifax Town FC are sifting through the faxed CVs of available footballers and tucking into lunch, a takeaway from Burger King. The senior man is a 61-year-old Scot called George Mulhall. Known as the Bullet when he hugged the left wing in the same Sunderland team as Brian Clough, Mulhall is fingering an old Manchester United programme from the final day of the 1968 season. His winner that afternoon deprived United of the league title.

The player-assistant-manager is Kieran O'Regan, a 35-year-old Irishman who might pass for Mulhall's son. As he steps up to shake hands, the first thing that strikes you about O'Regan is that the passing years have been kind to the boyish good looks that once caused the legendary Brighton manager, Jimmy Melia, to remark: 'O'Regan looks so young that he was thrown off the team bus last week because the driver thought he was only 12.'

The smile with which O'Regan greets me stays in place for almost all of the interview and there is an air of giddiness about the whole place. After ten games of the season, the 66-1 outsiders are top of the league, with eight victories, two draws and no defeats. Making his way towards a seat in the stand, O'Regan adopts the convenient shorthand of the professional footballer. 'Been brilliant, it has.'

In the city of Cork, in the early '80s, Kieran O' Regan was a minor celebrity. Thumb through the local newspapers from the period, and his name is writ large through his exploits with Tramore Athletic. Here, he is a 17-year-old substitute scoring an extra-time winner in the 1981 Intermediate Cup final. There, he is curling a 30-yard free-kick as his team won their second FAI youths cup final in just three seasons. Everywhere, he seems to figure in the small print of some success or other. Back then, Tramore boasted many prodigious talents but Dave Barry and O'Regan were the two finest. One stayed at home, and became the dual Gaelic football/ soccer star of an era; the other went to Brighton and Hove Albion to live out his dream.

Within only 12 months of departing Ireland, O'Regan came as close as he ever would to playing on Broadway. Towards the end of his first season at the Goldstone Ground, during a campaign that saw the club relegated, he made his first and only appearance in the old Division One. The game came a week before Brighton took on Manchester United in the 1983 FA Cup final and when Brighton's first choice right-back, Chris Ramsay, was injured in the drawn match, speculation mounted that O'Regan might play in the replay.

'There was a lot of hype about that, especially in the Irish papers, but the manager, Jimmy Melia, thought better of it. I still don't have any regrets about that. I did get to travel with the official party to Wembley, and God knows what might have happened to me if I had played. I might have had a nightmare and never recovered.'

Stoicism of that nature has served O'Regan well in a career that, after Brighton, took in Swindon Town, Huddersfield Town and West Bromwich Albion. On the way to becoming a veteran of over 300 first team games, he became inured to the iniquities of the professional game. In Cork city, O'Regan was a big fish in a small pool, and a precedent for his fellow citizens, Denis Irwin and Roy Keane; in England he discovered that both the other fish and the pool were that bit bigger.

'I was out of contract at Huddersfield once, and they asked me to go on a pre-season tour to the Isle of Man. I said that I wasn't going anywhere until my contract was signed. So they sent me out playing with the youth team. There's me and ten kids playing the likes of Eccles Hill miners' welfare in charity games. That kind of thing happens all the time to professionals and is hardly ever reported.'

For all that, Huddersfield was still mostly a happy memory. Initially signed by the former Irish manager, Eoin Hand, he played in 10 different positions including stand-in goalkeeper during his five years there. It was while at Huddersfield too that he met his fiancée, Helen, and purchased his current home, a house in the village of Holmfirth that has been immortalised in the television series *Last of the Summer Wine*. After those relative highs, West Brom represented a new low.

A disagreement with the manager, Keith Burkinshaw, precipitated a lengthy exile from the first team and prolonged exposure to the vicissitudes of the game. 'I went from being a regular first team player – even captain on occasions – to being a complete nobody. The very worst came when Keith organised an 11-a-side practice match one morning, and virtually all the fit playing staff were involved. But for some reason best known to himself, he left me out. I was standing on the touchline watching when he walked past me and said: "Can't get a game then, Kieran?" I went to see him a few times but it got to the stage where I couldn't see any future for myself at the Hawthorns.'

Recalled to the first team for the first game after Burkinshaw had been sacked, O'Regan was eventually released on a free transfer. 'Of course, you feel like a bit of a failure when that happens, but then you realise there are 6- or 700 players let go like that every summer. We have a young lad here called Jamie Patterson who was released by Scunthorpe in May, and there are a load of scouts chasing him now. Just because one manager doesn't fancy you, doesn't mean you're not any good.'

In footballing limbo, O'Regan's immediate options were limited to a chance to play in Hong Kong or the opportunity to train with Halifax. 'I came down here and they were very nice to me from the off. They sorted me out a contract and the chairman, John Stockwell, said he'd give me a job in his textile company. That was a good offer because like so many other footballers, I hadn't acquired any skills away from the game. I tried a couple of times. I even went to night school one season but I couldn't hack it. I'd been away from it too long.'

Halifax Town's past is described as colourful rather than miserable, in the same way that somebody who is diagnosed with a terminal illness decides they will laugh rather than cry. Nobody typified the club's peculiar brand of gallows humour better than one former manager, John McGrath. 'The three most used words in football are Halifax Town nil,' he quipped during one particular crisis. On another occasion, he deflected attention from whichever disaster was pending by pointing out that Benny the club cat was complaining that too many mice in the ground were dying of starvation.

It certainly says something about the club that in an 87-year existence, its most notable entry in the record books is that it holds the joint record for worst ever defeat – 13-0 against Stockport County in 1934. The name is forever associated too with a host of other unseemly columns like lowest crowds, longest run without a goal and most number of re-elections to the Football League. Embarrassing, sure, but small beer compared to the time three years ago when pressing VAT and tax bills took them within one week of liquidation.

In the spring of 1997, they looked set for more ignominy. With three months left in their Vauxhall Conference campaign, they were candidates for relegation to the Unibond Premier League, another giant step down football's food chain. Enter the caretaker management team of George Mulhall and Kieran O'Regan. 'I just agreed when I was asked. It is a big challenge even at this level,' says O'Regan. 'The lads were rock bottom and the side was really leaking goals but we were told that if we kept the team in the Conference, there was a chance we'd be given the job permanently.' So it proved.

On the final day of last season, Halifax needed a win against Stevenage to avoid relegation. With only two minutes left, a 3-2 lead became 4-2 and the future was suddenly secure. 'I've played in every division and been on some good teams, but nothing meant as much to me as that. I hadn't been as emotional about anything since I won my first Irish cap.'

The fact that money is tight doesn't diminish the sense of fulfilment. O'Regan and Mulhall are part-time employees with a full-time passion. Mulhall spends most of his days there while O'Regan pops in on his breaks from the local textile mill. The resurgence of their team is testimony to their commitment and their canny dealings. As a club that has only recently ventured back into the black, they have assembled a side consisting mainly of free transfers, previously untried youngsters and loan players. Occasionally they will splash out on a new signing, but their most auspicious purchase, Patterson, cost just £8,000. In a league where the richer clubs have been known to pay ten times that for a striker, they have to know what they're doing.

Their cause has been helped by the odd stroke of luck to shore up the Halifax defence, like procuring Brian Kilcline, the man who captained Coventry City to their FA Cup victory in 1988. Kilcline wasn't so much bought as found. A Halifax fan was doing some plumbing at Kilcline's house when he inquired as to whether the bearded giant was still playing. On discovering that he wasn't, the plumber made a call to George Mulhall. In the week that the team had lost their previous centre-half, Peter Jackson, to the Huddersfield manager's job, it was perhaps their luckiest break.

Kilcline's trademark – abrupt defending – provides a contrast to the otherwise pure footballing sensibilities of the team. They play a three-five-two formation, the duties of sweeper often falling to O'Regan, and are adamant that they are one of the best football-playing teams in the league. For a small club located in the hinterland of Manchester and Leeds, the only way of gaining support is to play attractive football. That Halifax's investment in this policy is paying off can be gauged by the fact that games which attracted 6- or 700 last season are being witnessed by gates of over 1500 this time round.

At this level, the relationship between gate receipts and money available to buy players is paramount, because even in the Conference, there are the haves and have-nots. Rushden and Diamonds, Halifax's main rivals for promotion all season, are backed by the £220m fortune of Max Griggs, the proprietor of Dr Marten's. Beside their stadium, Rushden have a purpose-built astroturf facility, and another grass pitch for training. Halifax Town's desire to preserve the excellent surface at the Shay means they have their twice-weekly work-outs at a local school.

The constant struggle invigorates O'Regan even if it might all have worked out differently than it has. Between the ages of 19 and 21, he was capped four times by Ireland. The prime of his career coincided with his country's most successful spell, and yet he was never seen in an Irish jersey again after 1986. Does he lament the direction his career has taken? Not at all.

'I'm happy with what I've achieved in my career. I remember when I was 15, myself and Dave Barry went over to Glasgow Celtic for a week's trial, a great experience for two boys from Cork. Anyway, Celtic were playing at home against Morton that Saturday and after the match, I asked the assistant manger John Clark, a Lisbon lion, if he would get the players to sign my programme.

'With that, he brought me inside the door and sat me down next to Danny McGrain. It was an unbelievable feeling. If you'd have said to me then, you can go to England, play as a full-time professional in the league for 12 years and then do what I'm doing now for Halifax Town, I would have said: "That'll do for me." '

Time is moving on and O'Regan's other responsibilities are waiting. The chairman is a lenient boss, but best not take too much advantage. Leaving him to his job at the textile mill that Wednesday afternoon, he was talking about his side's chances of an FA Cup run. At that stage, they were two games away from the first round proper. 'If we were to get that far, and maybe draw somebody like Burnley, we'd be guaranteed they'd bring 5,000 or 6,000 to the game. That kind of cash would allow us to stay overnight for a couple of the away games down in London, or maybe buy a new player.'

The FA Cup run never materialised. Stevenage would carry the Conference banner into the further reaches of the competition, but Halifax barely noticed. They had other fish to fry. On 21 March, they beat Rushden and Diamonds 2-0 at The Shay to move 13 points clear at the top of the table. The game was all ticket. Twelve days later, the newly revamped stadium, complete with £700,000 worth of improvements paid for by the club, the council and Halifax Blue Sox, was passed fit after an inspection by officials of the Football League. A couple of weeks later, they clinched the title and promotion back to Division Three.

In June, a decision was made to revert to full-time status and Kieran O'Regan was back in the game.

Crossing the forecourt of the Arnold Clark garage in Perth, moving between a row of shiny, new Alfa Romeos, you ask a man in a suit where you might find John Donegan. He points you in the direction of a windowless building at the back. At the far end of it, Donegan is hunched over a Fiat Punto with a cloth in his hand. Spotting your approach, he wipes his hand on his overalls before extending it in welcome. The shake is firm as you'd expect a goalkeeper's to be.

The accent still reeks of north Cork. Four years in the west of Scotland have hardly diluted it at all, and driving up the hill towards his house he pronounces the Irish for Mitchelstown with a degree of relish instilled by a Christian Brothers' education: 'Baile Mhisteala'. Sometimes his mother mocks him saying that Scottish phrases have insinuated their way into his vocabulary but he has his own defence for that. 'Sure, what can you do, when you're living among these people every day of your life, you're bound to pick things up.'

John Donegan left Ireland at 19 to pursue a career as a professional footballer. Seven years later, this is where he's at. Five days a week, he valets cars for Arnold Clark; on Saturdays, he keeps goal for Forfar Athletic in the Scottish Second Division. A footnote in the greater scheme of things, their ground, Station Park, seats 739 although it's rare enough that every seat is filled. They pay their players a basic match fee of £30 and treble that amount if they win. In a good season, a Forfar player can take home five or six grand. The Premiership, this is not.

'The money isn't great but you play because you want to play and you love to play. The club make sure that you're never out of pocket for travelling expenses and it's just handy to get a few bob for playing football. If I wasn't getting any money for it, I'd still be playing for somebody. It's only a 35-mile drive up for me but there are other fellas making a 200-mile round trip from Glasgow just to get a game. They're hardly in it for the money.'

They do things differently down here. Only two years ago, Forfar brought a 15-year-old boy on as a substitute in one game, and it's not unusual for a key player to miss a fixture through work commitments. Normal rules simply do not apply. During a spell out of the team last season, Donegan was sitting on the bench as third sub when an outfield player was injured. With the other two subs already used, they had no problem putting him into midfield.

'The pressure is nothing here. This is about enjoyment, and I'm enjoying it now more than I ever did as a full-time professional. Don't get me wrong, I still go out and play hard on a Saturday. I'm out there swearing mad with me elbows flying all over the place. But it's not the be-all and end-all.'

Donegan is sitting in the front room of the maisonette he shares with his Scottish wife Lisa. The walls are hung with photographs of their wedding and a framed reproduction of the 1916 Proclamation of Irish Independence. Upstairs, he's converted one of the spare rooms into a gym and his lean, angular physique speaks volumes for how often he uses it. He is friendly and articulate, and for a man whose career is in many ways a classic tale of what might have been, anything but bitter.

At 18, Cork City pitched Donegan into the away leg of a Cup Winnners' Cup match against Torpedo Moscow. They lost 5-0, but nobody blamed the rookie keeper for that. Back then, Donegan was one of City's representatives on a government-sponsored soccer course which ran for five days a week in Palmerstown, west Dublin. Every Monday morning, he travelled from Cork to Dublin on the train with, amongst other hopefuls, Roy Keane.

The first of its kind in Ireland, the programme was

designed to improve the best young Irish players who weren't already playing in England or Scotland. If Keane is the most famous graduate, the majority of the class still ply their trade in the National League of Ireland. 'I would never look at Roy Keane, and say that should be me there – you can't live your life like that. Fair play to him for everything he's achieved. He worked hard enough for it.'

Donegan's own performances on the FAS course earned him a move to Kilkenny City and it was while playing at Buckley Park that he caught the eye of Millwall and Derby County. Millwall made the first offer, and he didn't want to take a chance on waiting for Derby to come back. If he had waited, would he be somewhere else now?

'If I had my time again, I would have stayed at Kilkenny until the end of the season, and waited for a team to come in that would have given me a more favourable deal. The money was fine at Millwall but there were a few ould things that I could have got put into my contract. I didn't get them in because I didn't have the experience of dealing with an English club, and I felt if I turned down the chance, I might not get another.'

At Millwall, things went well for the first year and a half. A regular in a reserve team peopled by the likes of Chris Armstrong, he sat on the first team bench waiting his chance. Torn ligaments in his hand meant that opportunity never quite knocked and by the time he'd recovered properly from the injury, two other keepers had leapfrogged him in the reckoning. As part of his rehabilitation, Millwall farmed him out on loan to Dulwich Hamlet of the Diadora League.

'That was a great experience. The standard down there was quite good as there were a lot of older professionals playing. It gave me the chance to get games under me belt and the regular first team football improved me.' But not enough to impress Millwall. At the end of his contract, he was released and, exposed to the harsh reality of the unemployed footballer, he began circulating CVs to every club he could think of. Nothing came of those until a contact at Millwall arranged a trial for him at St Johnstone.

His first season at McDiarmid Park went well. He felt the club manager, John McLelland, rated him, and again he saw his chance coming sooner, rather than later. Before it could, however, McLelland was replaced by Paul Sturrock, and the new boss didn't have the same taste in goalkeepers as the old one. Donegan found himself surplus to requirements again. Six months before his contract was up, they told him he could leave. Cue the uglier side of the beautiful game.

'Sturrock told me he wanted to pay me off. I said fine as long as he would give me decent money. He offered me six weeks wages and I was looking for six months. I told him that I was going nowhere for that money and he banned me from training with the club.' For six months, Donegan collected his wages and tried to keep fit. He even headed back to Cork for a month to clear his head. Then, a chance meeting with a Forfar official in a Perth pub brought a change of luck. Forfar said he could train with them until he was eligible again and as soon as he became a free agent, they signed him.

'It would have been nice to stay professional but I decided if I had to step down to play first team, so be it. I thought too that maybe somebody might see me here and come in for me. I still think like that a bit, although I'm probably too old now, it's probably all over for me. I've been lucky in sport, though, in that I've played in Fitzgerald Stadium in Killarney before 40,000 and even played at the Melbourne Cricket Ground in Australia.

'I've had great experiences and big thrills but I have no problems getting going for games here. There might be only 500 in the ground but you can hear every one of them shouting at ya. With 40,000, you can't hear a thing. I get to hear every 'Donegan, ya effin eejit'. It's probably just as well there's only 500 at the games, that means I can only fall out with 500.'

Fitzgerald Stadium and the MCG give clues to Donegan's past. In a previous life, he was a Gaelic football prodigy. Growing up in Mitchelstown, a market town in north Cork where at school he remembers, 'GAA was like a religion', Donegan was a willing acolyte. If he wasn't playing Gaelic football for the school, he was travelling the province playing handball alongside his brothers. Two years running, he made the Cork minor Gaelic football team and when the county sent a squad of 17-year-olds to Australia in 1988, Donegan's only rival for the accord of most valuable player was Colin Corkery.

At the end of the trip, both players were heavily courted by Australian Rules clubs. Corkery signed on for a couple of years before coming home to become a regular on the Cork senior football team and an All-Star. Donegan decided that soccer was a more realistic prospect for a career in professional sport than a game that's played with an oval ball. Any regrets?

'No, see, I never dreamt of being a professional footballer, never even thought about it once growing up. I only played in goal for the local soccer team, Park United, because that's the only position where I could get my game. I would have been happy just playing Gaelic football at home in Mitchelstown. Then somebody asked me to play League of Ireland, and I realised I could make a career in soccer. In all the years since, that time when I went back to Cork for a month is the only time I ever thought about giving this up. I'm the kind of fella who will always try and go as far as I can with something, and it's been a nice journey. I'm absolutely delighted playing for Forfar and I love living in Perth. My wife Lisa is pregnant with our first child. I'm happy as Larry.'

The interview ends abruptly with an apology. 'I have to mosey.' A glance at his watch tells Donegan that half past one is fast approaching, and he needs to be back at work. Arnold Clark himself often pops his head in on Mondays, so best not take any chances with being late. As his car approaches the garage, he insists on dropping his passenger the extra 300 yards around the corner to the train station.

'If I'm a few minutes late so what, they owe me that much. Like, I could have got other jobs in the last year but none where I could get the time off work to play football. Anyway, I quite like the job and I know an awful lot more about cars now than I did before.'

Happy with the job, content with life and thrilled at the prospect of becoming a father, his car exits the station with a beep of the horn and a cheery smile. Off up the road to work. John Donegan, goalkeeper, car valet, happy as Larry.

Two weeks after our meeting, Forfar lost 4-0 to Livingstone and began a slide down the table that brought them from flirting with the prospect of promotion to the brink of relegation. The defeat marked the end of Donegan's sojourn in the first team. 'The manager, Ian McPhee, called me in and told me he was making a change after that game. I told him that it wasn't fair to scapegoat the goalkeeper for the defeat but he disagreed.' Donegan spent the rest of the season on the bench, and at the end of it, he refused the club's offer of a new contract. Nobody in Ireland ever dreams of playing for Forfar Athletic.

Chapter Three

Scouting for glory

'Scouts don't scout in order to get rich. They scout because they know and because they're opinionated men. You could fire them all and hire scientists and buy machines and you'd wind up with lots of numbers, and not too many recommendations where a guy is ready to put his individual ass on the line. It's a unique job.'
DOLLAR SIGN ON THE MUSCLE, KEVIN KERRANE, 1989

I Our man on the motorbike

A Sunday morning in Fairview Park on the northside of Dublin city and this parcel of land, sandwiched between the main road and the railway line, is playing host to a number of games. A man in a furry hat is standing on the sideline, casting his eye over an Under-15 schoolboys' game between Belvedere Boys and Stella Maris. His cream and black jacket with the Liver bird logo on the breast betrays the reason for his presence. Four years ago, Liverpool FC charged Noel McCabe with unearthing the next batch of Irish talent, and this morning he's busy prospecting.

McCabe came to Liverpool with something of a reputation, recommended to their director of youth development, Steve Heighway, by Ronnie Whelan, with Roy Keane as the most celebrated entry in his CV. One Sunday morning seven years ago, at this very venue, McCabe, then in the employ of Nottingham Forest, took note of Keane playing on the pitch next to this one in an FAI Youths Cup match and begot a legend.

'Even though his team were beaten 4-0 by Belvedere, he was constantly getting on the ball, trying to make things happen. He had tremendous heading ability too, and when in possession, he wanted to go past people, and most times he was beating them with ease.' No scout had ever believed enough in Keane before but when McCabe sat down to compile his report that evening, he was effusive in his praise.

ROY KEANE: AGE 18

Roy is a player who in this game showed he has good skill and vision in finding players with his passes. He is progressive with his tackling and was involved in activity around the middle of the park. His pace is very good and he loved taking on players and going for the back line – and could get good crosses in. He looks a nice, balanced player and his upper body is broad and appears a very strong player. He is, in my opinion, a player to go on trial to Forest right away.

That report is neatly filed away in a blue folder, the covers of which conceal information on just about every promising Irish player of the last decade. The names speak for themselves.

DAMIEN DUFF: AGE 15

Damien is not tall but is very skilful on the ball. He is very intelligent with the ball and his left foot was a treat. He is the kind of boy who would have to go to England at 16 years of age and spend two or three seasons finding out if he is going to become a player with training etc . . .

GARETH FARRELLY: AGE 15

Farrelly had a quiet game. He had to chase the game nearly all through. He didn't have as much of the ball as Belvedere but when he received the ball, he was effective with his passing. *The players around him would not be anything compared with his international colleagues at this level, probably the reason for the quiet game.*

MARK KENNEDY: AGE 15
Kennedy was by far the best player on view. His skill on the ball was not unlike Gary Crosby (former Nottingham Forest winger). When he gets on the ball, he wants to take on players and go by them with a bit of confidence. He scored the equaliser for his team and was a constant threat to the opposition.

ALAN MAYBURY: AGE 15
Alan is a very quick player who loved to break from the back with a lot of success in taking on players and going by them with great pace. He reads the game very well indeed against a team who is unbeaten and regarded by me as the best under-15 team in the country. I strongly recommend Alan for a trial with Liverpool FC right away.

JASON SHERLOCK: AGE 16
I feel the player Sherlock is by far the best under-16 player in Ireland today. He is very quick and has special skill in taking on players, all done at speed with the ball. He is a must for you to look at. His goals are special. I saw him score two while he was on for 25 minutes. There was no occasion for him to show his heading ability in this game. But, what he did with the ball on the ground was enough.

Discovering Keane gained McCabe huge kudos. A succession of journalists and even TV cameras have been to his house to hear the story of how he unearthed that gem. But the fame brought with it a degree of notoriety that has made his job more difficult. In 1992, his wooing of Mark Kennedy was hampered by the first real bout of Keane hysteria and in the kerfuffle that ensued, Mick McCarthy snatched Kennedy away for Millwall. McCabe, growing reputation and all, could hardly compete with Captain Fantastic calling around to the Kennedy house.

Everton's Gareth Farrelly was another whom McCabe had on the way to Forest until a trip to Aston Villa, then home to McGrath, Townsend, Staunton and Houghton persuaded the youngster otherwise. 'I learned the hard way about how quickly young players change their minds. After a while, you don't get upset. You see, footballers are like buses. You regret missing one but there'll always be another one along in a minute.'

Losing out on Kennedy and Farrelly, who both confirmed his initial faith by becoming senior internationals, hurt McCabe but there were other incidents that scarred him more. One teenager, who had been to Forest on a week's training, changed his mind in suspicious circumstances. A month after, when the boy began his career at another English club, McCabe's suspicions were confirmed. Walking past the boy's house, he saw that it had been extensively refurbished, replete with aluminium windows. Knowing the club in question's propensity for throwing money about, McCabe did not think the two incidents unrelated.

Although neither Forest nor Liverpool have ever believed in using such inducements, others are not so moral about dangling cash in front of gifted youngsters and their parents. Richie Partridge, one of four McCabe protégés currently at Anfield is a case in point. Despite pledging himself to Liverpool from the age of 15, Partridge's family were forced to change their telephone number twice before finally going ex-directory as some English clubs wouldn't take no for an answer. The phone calls to the Partridge house included one request to name their price and another promise to buy them a house in England near their son.

By way of competition, the only thing McCabe could offer was a trip on the Liverpool team bus when they came to Lansdowne Road to play UCD. In the dressing-room, Partridge was introduced to all the first team players and given little tasks like doling out cups of tea. Afterwards, they gave him some free gear and he was utterly smitten. The same night, he returned home and dismantled the Manchester United shrine in his bedroom.

'Liverpool don't offer anything except their good name,

and a promise to be honest in their dealings. From the moment a boy arrives at the club, a daily log is kept about his movements and activities. They record what time he got up, what time he went to bed, how he performed in training and everything he did in between.'

Thirty-three years ago, Noel McCabe founded Belvedere Boys FC with Vinny Butler, and soccer has consumed him ever since. It was Ray Treacy who first nominated him for a scouting position with Oxford United – Paul Byrne was the first player he sent across – and 11 years later, McCabe's weekly itinerary might include as many as ten games.

A couple of years ago, kidney problems precipitated his early retirement from the Department of Health, and he's been able to devote even more time to his task. 'I've always been more or less full-time in football. People who know me will tell you that I have no desire for exotic holidays or fancy things or any stuff like that. All I've ever been interested in is football.'

His is an existence that thrives on gossip and tip-offs. A network of contacts all over the country send McCabe newspaper clippings or ring him with the latest tattle about latent talents. Acting on information received, he takes off all over the country. 'I went down to this dirt-track in Roscommon once but the boy wasn't up to standard. I told him I'd go to see him again the next time his club were playing in Dublin. Later that day, I was standing on the street, waiting for the bus to Dublin when he came along asking me to come down again next weekend. Telling him that I couldn't, that was the hardest part.'

During his time working for Forest, McCabe was known to Brian Clough and the rest of the staff at the City Ground as 'Our man on the motorbike.' He's long since given up the bike, and buses and trains are his modes of transport now. From his home in Donnycarney, he traipses around Dublin, and the rest of the country, in pursuit of the one player a year he will sign for Liverpool. Journeys home are for reflecting on each part of a boy's personality to see if he adds up to a genuine contender.

'A lot of boys in this country are spoilt. They think they're better than they actually are. When I first met Roy Keane, the minute we started talking, I knew that he was desperate to go cross-channel. He was so hungry for it that I reckon he would have swum across to England if I asked him to. I loved that.'

During his initial conversations with young players and their parents, Noel McCabe likes to stress how difficult it will be for the boy to make it at the highest level. He makes a gesture with his thumb and forefinger, and tells them: 'This is how much of a chance you have.' Nobody yet has thought those odds too small.

II Field of dreams

The night sky over Shinrone is black and blue and promising rain. The wind is whipping in from the west, and huddled in the bleakness of the parish hall car park, there are 20 soccer players and five cars. John Freeman moves among them breezily, a few strands of hair dragged across his balding pate and the white lines of his Walsall FC tracksuit glowing in the dark. All the while, his upbeat banter strains to warm the mood on a chilly evening in February.

It's after 7 p.m. when Billy Kavanagh's car swishes across the gravel. Billy unlocks the door of a tiny, wooden hut, trips some switches and at ten-second intervals, the floodlight pylons in each corner of an Offaly field ignite. As the perfect outline of a soccer pitch forms in the near distance, it's like a scene from the baseball movie *Field of Dreams*. Even if in Hollywood one of the pylons wouldn't be giving trouble on the night, the fantasy motif is not out of kilter with the mood.

John Freeman runs a sports trophy shop in Thurles and does a neat line in fostering the soccer talent of middle Ireland. Of the 20 players following him down the muddy track that leads towards the dressing-room this Wednesday night, eight have been on trials at English clubs; two of them have already agreed terms; the rest are the Shinrone junior team which he manages. He doesn't like to use the term himself but some people would call this a school of excellence.

Shinrone is a village in the heart of hurling country. Offaly have contested two of the last five All Ireland hurling finals, and only two hundred yards through the fields lies the border with Tipperary, a county which likes to identify itself as 'the home of hurling'. According to the stereotypes, this shouldn't really be fecund territory for the soccer gospel but John Freeman's experience has shown him otherwise.

John Dawson and Dinny Nevin are sitting in a car, taking shelter from the night and eavesdropping a radio signal of England versus Italy that hisses and crackles too much for comfort. While their minds are at Wembley, their sons Danny and Fergus are lapping the field in front of them, listening to the instructions of Freeman.

It was six months ago when Danny Dawson read a piece in a newspaper about Freeman's scouting activities. At that time, Danny was already a veteran of writing letters to English clubs looking for trials. None of them took the trouble to reply to a youngster from Kilfinnane, County Limerick. Newspaper clipping in hand, Danny sat down and dashed off a note to Freeman. A couple of days later, he received an invitation to spend a night in Shinrone, and he hasn't missed a week since. Neither has his Dad.

'I came in from work tonight, gobbled down my dinner and got straight into the car,' says John Dawson. 'It's 80 miles over and 80 back but it flies in because all Danny talks about is soccer. In fact, it's all I can remember him talking about nearly since he could talk. As long as he's got a chance at his dream, I'll take him wherever he needs to go.'

In January 1997, Danny Dawson spent a week on trial at Stockport County. It wasn't the Premiership and it definitely wasn't Liverpool, the club of his dreams, but it was a start. Fergus Nevin accompanied him on that trip and is cut from the same cloth.

Dinny Nevin used to scoff at his son's talk of a career in professional football. 'Since he was in national school I've been warning him that soccer players didn't get spotted in places like Terryglass, County Tipperary. It's only the fellas from the big cities that get picked up.' One Sunday morning in 1996, John Freeman happened upon a Shannon Rangers

69

game on the shores of Lough Derg, and Fergus Nevin chose to shine that day. Dinny Nevin doesn't scoff anymore – he's too busy doing the driving.

Freeman took a circuitous route to the fringes of the professional game. In a previous life, he was the chairman of the St Patrick's hurling club in Thurles, the birthplace of the Gaelic Athletic Association in 1884. It was the late '70s, and Freeman prided himself on being something of an innovator. At a time when Tipperary hurling was on its uppers, he imported outside coaches like Justin McCarthy and Pat Henderson for training sessions. After devices like that failed to attract the youngsters in sufficient numbers, he implemented more drastic measures.

His first major initiative was a fund-raising venture involving a seven-a-side soccer tournament. The competition was advertised openly in the local paper, *The Tipperary Star*, and one anonymous reader sent a copy of the advert to members of the county board in an attempt to provoke action against the club. Despite the protestations of some, the board decided against punishing St Patrick's for their action. Buoyed by this, Freeman went a step further.

'Because there was so much soccer on television, we felt that our youngsters were drifting away from hurling to soccer. We decided that if we got them out to play soccer in the winter, then they'd stay with us to play hurling in the summer. So we started a six-a-side soccer league and suddenly we couldn't cope with the numbers that we were getting.'

No doubt the interest in soccer was just waiting to be tapped into but in a further enticement, Freeman ran a scheme of bonus payments whereby the leading goalscorer in the final received £2 while all other scorers were paid £1. Twenty-odd years later, as the GAA grapples with the onset of some form of semi-professionalism, it's safe to say the financial inducement was an idea ahead of its time.

The scheme was a roaring success, and almost 160 boys participated in the first competition. Since the club had lost its own ground to property developers, the final, between

'Leeds United' and 'Spurs' was played on the outside pitch at Semple Stadium, the most hallowed venue in hurling lore. The players gained entry by squeezing through the main gate, the bolt on which was loose enough to allow one person to slip through at a time. With dressing-room facilities denied them, the boys togged out on the side of the pitch and when it came to marking out the ground, they improvised: iron bars for goalposts and upturned hurleys for corner-flags.

In January 1977, after one of its journalists, Seamus Martin, received an anonymous tip-off which he felt was designed to harm St Patrick's, the *Evening Herald* ran an article about the tournament. Enamoured of their twin struggles to find their own ground and to keep hold of the sporting imagination of the town's youth, Martin wrote a very positive piece. He felt that their methods were 'unorthodox but sincere' and that the youngsters 'showed a great deal of football skill for lads who had never received any real coaching in the game.'

The publicity proved the beginning of the end. Some time earlier, Freeman was told it would be all right to continue with the soccer provided it wasn't advertised. In the aftermath of Martin's article, the St Patrick's club were found guilty of 'Being involved in the promotion of games other than those of Gaelic football, hurling and handball.' Sixty-four of the youngsters were suspended from the GAA for six months and the executive committee of the club, including Freeman, were placed under indefinite suspension.

After further wrangling with the disciplinary structures of the GAA over a period of two years, Freeman and his brother Dermot were suspended from the association for five years with no further affiliation to be accepted from the club. That was 1979 and if he has looked back since, it is only to see how far he's come. 'My biggest piece of luck ever was being banned by the GAA. It was the makings of me.'

In his first year at the helm of St Patrick's soccer club, Freeman made contact with Maurice Newman at Crystal Palace. Soon after that, Liam Durack and Patrick Gleeson made the trip from Thurles to Selhurst Park. In the scrapbook where he keeps the cuttings which document his life in sport, there is a yellowing newspaper photo of Durack and Gleeson, flanked on either side by Clive Allen and Terry Venables.

There were other protégés throughout the '80s, and though none of them quite made the grade, it didn't take much encouragement to keep him going. When a neighbour's child, Alan Carey, made his first team début for Reading in 1994, Freeman knew the work he was doing was worthwhile. It was about the same time that Shinrone took Freeman on as their manager, and he decided to use the floodlit Wednesday evenings to run the rule over various prospects from within a 100-mile radius.

Word quickly seeped out about the opportunities available, and sometimes hopefuls would arrive unannounced. One night, a boy and his father made the trek cross-country all the way from Cavan. If, like that boy, a lot of them didn't make the grade, nobody was ever turned away without getting a fair chance to shine.

Some utilise the opportunity better than others. Shane Fogarty is a gangling teenager, the only boy in Templetuohy with a boot deal. Out of school uniform, he dresses from head to toe in Patrick sportswear, courtesy of Asport in Donegal. From the age of 14, he has been over and back to Walsall. The Walsall youth team manager, a former Northern Ireland youth team manager called Eric McManus, even went as far as providing Freeman with a training programme specific to Fogarty's needs.

Freeman doesn't mind taking on board the advice of others. He has no coaching badges himself, all he brings to this task is an eye for talent and the kind of infectious enthusiasm that means he's last to leave the field every Wednesday night. Billy Kavanagh will testify to that.

This night, as the clock ticks towards half past nine, Billy is anxious to clear the car-park so he can close up. One by one the players are piling into cars or setting off on foot with an encouraging word from Freeman ringing in their ears. When Kavanagh re-opens the tiny, wooden hut in the corner, he trips the switches again. This time, the lights go out and the soccer pitch evaporates back into the darkness, out of sight. But not out of their dreams.

After that first February meeting, the phone calls came thick and fast from John Freeman. 'I've got loads more coming to me now, there's so many interested that I don't know how to handle it' he once said breathlessly. Each time he'd ring, he'd have updated information about the progress of his individual charges. In December, he was thrilled when Alan Carey, his first real graduate, scored for Basingstoke in the FA Cup second round against Northampton, and was interviewed on *Match of the Day* afterwards. 'The number of people coming in to the shop all week to talk to me about it has been amazing.'

Later that month, the news was even better. Fergus Nevin, the tidy full-back who stood out one morning on the shores of Lough Derg, signed a two-year contract with Plymouth Argyle. He was followed in quick succession to the same club by Shane Fogarty who felt he'd be happier going to a club where there was already another Irish boy in situ. For Freeman's field of dreams, the first harvest is imminent.

III The wanderer

When Pat Devlin was 15 years old, his scoring exploits with St Joseph's Boys in the Dublin schoolboys' league brought him to the attention of a couple of scouts. The representatives of Coventry City and Wolves were eager to get him across to England for trials but he was less enamoured of the prospect. 'This guy who wanted me to go to Coventry called out to my house, and I wouldn't go home while he was there. I hid around the corner until he left. I just wanted to get on with playing for Joey's. It never even entered my head to want to play in England.'

Thirty-four years later, it is Devlin who, wearing the badge of Newcastle United, parks his jeep outside unfamiliar houses, and hopes that the prospect he is chasing has the courage to be present for his visit. Having previously worked as Republic of Ireland scout for Blackburn Rovers and Liverpool, he took up his present position in the summer of 1997. His first campaign with Newcastle has seen his reputation in the game hugely enhanced. Damien Duff's emergence as a player so talented that his own manager, Roy Hodgson, has compared him to George Best, has been one of the stories of the season, and for this, Devlin can take some credit.

'I saw Damien playing for Leicester Celtic at 13. He was this little wimp of a fella but I took a little note of him and said I'd come back. I went to see him again after he moved to Lourdes Celtic, and what I saw that day, I really liked. He was a good little player with a dreadful hands on his hips style that made you think he couldn't run. He was a very intelligent player. He could pass the ball smartly, could run at people or could out-think them. He had the skill, the movement, the pace and up here in the head he was so good. After seeing him that second time, I hung my hat on him.'

Devlin's passing mention of Duff to Kenny Dalglish was so effusive that the Blackburn manager was eager to see the boy play as quickly as possible, and the scout organised for the Irish Under-15s to play a friendly at Ewood Park. 'There was a big posse of people around Kenny that night, everybody was all over him trying to point out this player and that. So I went up the back of the stand on my own and at half-time, Kenny comes up to me and says: "The boy Duff is a player, we have to have him, and what about this lad Maybury?" Alan Maybury was already on his way to Leeds but we had Damien in our sights from there.'

Devlin is strangely reluctant to overstate his part in Duff's rise. 'Sometimes scouts get a lot of credit for discovering players but that's exaggerated. Talking about competition for players in Dublin city is ludicrous. You don't have to be Einstein to work out where the best players are playing, I mean the phone never stops ringing with information about guys. Anybody could have signed Damien Duff but you have to stick your neck out and say "I want him". And anyway, there's still an awful lot of luck involved when the player gets to the other side.'

In every fledgling career, luck seems to be the key ingredient, the great intangible which ensures that the language and tone of the experienced soccer scout is permanently stuck in neutral. Pat Devlin speaks of one player maybe going all the way or refers to another as a possible international, always refraining from the use of probables. He knows that there are no certainties, no talent too large to insulate a teenager against failure. The variables are too many, and have been seen too often before for the scout to commit himself to anything definite. Devlin may hang his hat on a player's potential but he doesn't give any cast-iron guarantees.

'In the early days, I would have been naïve enough to send a boy over and think to myself "Yeah, he can't fail." I found out though that it's a long job, it's not just a matter of getting the player from A to B. He's got to be right mentally, he's got to have the determination, and people on the other side have to fancy him. They have to give him the chance and have to look after him as you would a baby, really. And then, you know, sometimes you fancy a guy's abilities at 16 and find that he's gone backwards by the time he's 18 because for some reason or other, he can't hack it.

'But you can't be afraid of making those decisions. I don't fear making mistakes. In other words, I'll stick my neck out on something and if it doesn't work out, it doesn't work out. I'll do my best, and I will expect the player to do his best and on top of that I will expect the people at whichever club to do their best for him. At the end of the day, if we achieve something like that he'll become a good player and everybody's gained. But if he doesn't make it, we have to look and ask why, and there can be so many reasons.

'It could be homesickness or maybe a coach who doesn't like you. It's not as glamorous as most people think, it's sad in many ways being away from home. It's rough and tough but if you come through it, you'll be a better person for it. Football is like life, you have to get the bounce of the ball and if you get a bad result you have to get up again and make sure it goes your way the next time. Before, I used to think players had a 25 per cent chance of making it. Now I think it's improved to as much as 50-50 because the boys going over now are a lot tougher. They know more about the scene and are definitely more streetwise.'

Pat Devlin was born and bred in the port town of Dún Laoghaire, south Dublin. After cutting his teeth with St Joseph's Boys in Sallynoggin, one of the premier schoolboy clubs in Ireland, he enjoyed a distinguished career in junior football, which was bookended by a couple of spells in the League of Ireland with St Patrick's Athletic and Shamrock Rovers. All through, he was picking up coaching badges and experience as he went, and when Bray Wanderers entered the League of Ireland for the first time in 1984, they appointed Devlin as first team coach.

Before they had played their first league match, Bray scored a shock Leinster Senior Cup victory over Shamrock Rovers, the aristocrats of Irish soccer. It was a morale-boosting victory that was to have larger consequences for Devlin's own career. A week after the game, a letter of congratulations arrived in the post from Bob Paisley at Liverpool. Once the initial shock had subsided, Devlin decided to publish the letter in the next club programme to further improve the mood of the new club. That was a PR masterstroke in itself, but for him, the fun was only starting.

'I got a phone call one day, asking me to meet Ron Yeats. I went over to meet Ron and he asked me if I could help them out with some scouting over here. To be honest, I told him I didn't know whether I'd have the time, or whether I'd have exactly what they wanted. To cut a long story short, I said I'd do it for six months. I ended up doing it for six years, and it was a hard six years, I learned a huge amount, it was like serving an apprenticeship.

'At the start, there was a lot of ignorance on my part. I didn't know who was who and I developed my own methods very quickly. I decided I wouldn't send young kids over, 11- or 12-year-olds, like some scouts. I wouldn't get anyone to sign until he was 16 and would never discuss any financial packages until the kid decided he wanted to sign for the club. Then and only then, would I discuss the contract. That was my philosophy then and I've stuck with it and it's served me well to this day.'

David Collins was the first Devlin recommendation to be signed by Liverpool. Capped at every international level but senior, Collins was captain of the Liverpool reserves for a time, and was tipped by one Irish newspaper as the Irish player to watch in the '90s. Unable to make the next vital step at Anfield, Collins had a couple of seasons at Oxford United before coming back to play in Ireland.

If the Collins experience taught Devlin his first, harsh lesson about the scouting business, others quickly followed. More than once, the Liverpool coaches were unimpressed by quality players he sent their way. When Mark Kinsella made his full Irish début in March 1998, Devlin allowed himself a wry smile. Despite his repeated entreaties on Kinsella's behalf, Liverpool were nonplussed about the player's gifts and had let him pass. Middlesbrough's Alan Moore, another current Irish international, suffered a similar fate some years later.

'I found through those experiences that the most important thing is to be honest to the parents and the kid, and to stick by what you believe in. It shouldn't matter if another scout thinks he's a bad player. If you feel he's good, you have to follow that right through. Very early in my career, there was one particular player who sums up what I'm saying. We came out to have a look at him playing a schoolboy international, and we had committed ourselves very heavily to the player, and I'll never forget it, Ron Yeats was in my house having his tea beforehand, and Kenny Dalglish rang saying, you know, just make sure you don't lose this guy.

'So we went up to the game and the boy was dreadful, he was embarrassing, he was awful. We had two choices, to be very dishonest and run away from him or follow through. This was a real test, and I always remember Ron looking at me saying: "Jaysus, what do you think we should do now?" And I said, "Well I don't really think we can backtrack on this because if we do, we will lose out on our reputation, and the club will suffer badly, and we'll end up with egg on our faces." We had to back our hunch, and we did and unfortunately the boy didn't make it at Liverpool.'

In those early days, Devlin's only function was spotting the talent, and making subsequent arrangements for the player to visit Anfield for trials. Over the years and through the three clubs he's worked for, his role has evolved significantly and his approach now is far more hands-on. He is, in effect, a full-time buffer between the family and the club.

'I do everything for Newcastle, I did everything for Blackburn. In other words, I would take charge of you completely. I would service you. When your parents wanted to go over, I would look after the flights. When you want to come home, I would look after your flight. If you're short of gear, I would get you gear, if your parents are worried about anything, I would check it out. It's not a case of "see ya, bye bye." If you're homesick, it's me you would come to. If I thought there was a problem within the club, I would go straight to the top. I wouldn't mess around. I would go straight to Kenny, it's the only way I can work.'

The relationship between Kenny Dalglish and Pat Devlin has long since crossed the line between professional and personal. Everywhere Dalglish has gone, Devlin has followed soon after. After Dalglish's shock resignation as Liverpool manager, Devlin stayed in their employ until his departure was hastened by a row with Graeme Souness. Dalglish's successor accused Devlin of being instrumental in guiding Gary Tallon, a precocious Irish striker in the direction of Ewood Park instead of Anfield.

'Souness was wrong. I don't operate like that and as the argument went on with Souness, Kenny got in touch and asked me to come to Blackburn. I said no at first and didn't do it for a year. I just helped them out with a few bits and pieces, but he kept saying: "Come on, come with me," so in the end, I did.'

At the time Devlin switched allegiances, Blackburn were embarking on a massive rebuilding programme on and off the field. In tandem with the purchases of the likes of Alan Shearer et al, huge strides were being taken in putting in place a proper infrastructure to ensure that the next generation of Blackburn players would come from within. It was Devlin's task to establish a supply line of Irish talent and at one stage, close to a dozen young Irish players were on the books. Even now, there are seven players there whom he sent across.

The figures are impressive until one considers that only Duff and Shay Given have made it into the first team, and even Given was forced to move on in search of a regular starting spot. Some have come home while others have dropped down the divisions. Gary Tallon, for instance, now plays for Mansfield Town in Division Three. Devlin's critics like to use the high attrition rate against him, but he is defiant.

'All I would say is that I can look at all the boys who went over there and say they went to an excellent club, got a magnificent opportunity that they would never have got here and got very well paid for it. I don't have any regrets in sending them. The only regret I have is that they don't all make it. But if they all made it, I'd be the best talent-spotter in the world. As I said, it's all about being in the right place at the right time. The most pleasing thing for me is that I know that I've done everything I could for them. I didn't help Damien Duff any more than the rest of them.'

Devlin's pursuit of Damien Duff was textbook, monitoring his progress from age 13 onwards before finally pouncing. Getting Shay Given to Blackburn was an entirely different process. Initially, Devlin received a tip-off that Given was unhappy with a derisory contract renewal he'd been offered after his first year at Glasgow Celtic. He kept an eye on the situation and organised for a goalkeeping scout to watch Given play for Celtic in a tournament in Holland. Devlin wanted to be sure that Given was as good as he remembered him being when he played for Lifford Celtic.

Once Kenny Dalglish was appraised of the positive scout's report, Given became a target and as soon as he left Glasgow Celtic to return home to Donegal, Blackburn moved. 'Kenny was away on a pre-season tour to Norway or Sweden and he just told me to get the deal done because there were other clubs, including Manchester United, also on his trail. So we brought Shay and his father Seamus over to Blackburn. We'd been in negotiations all day and it got to the stage where two people, who were very influential in Blackburn at the time, said: "No, we can't give him what he wants".' I was caught in the middle and I said: "Kenny told me to do the deal and if we don't, the boy is going to back out. I've promised him something, and we have to deliver." So eventually, they gave him what he was asking for.'

That evening, Given was picked to play in a friendly for Blackburn reserves against a local non-league club. Devlin accompanied Seamus Given to the match but was surprised when the player's father insisted on watching from a vantage point directly behind his son's goal, thinking this might intimidate and put more pressure on the 18-year-old.

'Seamus just said to me, "Ah, it'll be no problem to my boy, no hassle." Anyway the game starts and the next minute, this fella comes through, Shay comes running out like a lunatic, and yer man pops it over him into the goal. I looked at the father and said, "That wasn't too clever, was it?" Seamus just says: "Don't worry about it, he'll make up for that."

'At that point, Jim Furnell, the Blackburn director of youth development and a former goalkeeper himself came over and asked if Shay had signed, so I was explaining to Jim that, you know, he was probably only nervous. With that, another ball comes in, Shay's not coming and then he's coming, and yer man pops it, and Shay's at fault. I turned to the father and said; "Whew, that's the second one, it's just as well we've signed the contract." Seamus says: "Ah he'll make up for that now, he'll make up for that."

'Soon after, another ball comes across down the right side, Shay takes a lunge out his left hand side to try and stop it, and bang, back of the net, I turned to Seamus, and said: "Seamus, do you have a good solicitor?" Remember now, this is not half-time yet, and he says: "I don't know what's wrong with him, he's not himself." At the break, they took him off and going back in the taxi, the driver, who's a Dubliner living over there, asked me how he'd done. So I start telling him the story and Seamus Given interrupts and says: "Enough of that; my boy will play for Ireland before he's 21.'"

Shay Given won his first Irish senior cap at the age of 19. Remembering the minutiae of Given's first outing in Blackburn's colours is the stuff of every scout's existence. These men have an encylopedic knowledge of the players who have passed through their hands, and even most of those who haven't. Devlin isn't big on report-writing, but in his head, he has files on every major Irish talent of the last decade. He's won the hand of some and lost more.

'Every club now is looking for the Robbie Keanes, the Damien Duffs, the Roy Keanes, but you've got to be fair across the board. We always went for quality not quantity. He has to be better than what they have over there, not just better than what is in Ireland. I don't think sending 10 or 12 players over, and hoping to get one out of it is fair. The other thing which I decided on is that if I sent you over and you were a right-back, I wasn't going to send another right-back over the following year. That was going to be unfair on you. It wouldn't give you enough time to come through.'

The world of scouting is a small one. Inevitably, the sharpest movers end up standing on the same sidelines, chasing the same players. Devlin likes to play down the competitive element of it all but knows that the petty rivalries do give off a whiff of rancour. Some scouts accept losing a player better than others and the often surreptitious nature of the profession means that it is rife with rumours and accusations.

'We had this boy who was about to sign for Blackburn. He was one of the best schoolboy players ever, and when he and his father were over talking to Kenny Dalglish, they were distraught because this other scout had been going around saying that the boy was on drugs and drinking. I was appalled by that and from then onwards, I decided to do what I think is right. I row my own boat and if I lay myself open for criticism, I should deserve it.

'I've heard the stories about people getting heating into their houses, or new cars. But I don't see that happening.

Maybe it does with the smaller clubs but hand on heart, I can say that all the parents ever get out of us is a trip to England, to the club. If a boy says he wants to sign we bring the parents over to wine and dine them before that. There are a lot of myths about scouting but I operate only within the rules and regulations, never outside them.'

In his first ten years as a scout, Devlin was paid expenses for his time. In the last two, he's put his role on a more professional footing, setting up in business as a full-time sports consultant who can boast Adidas among his clients. He combines this work with his part-time post as manager of Bray Wanderers. To spend some time with Devlin is to accompany a man on his personal journey from one-time painter and decorator cum junior footballer to the position where he has the ear of one of the most exalted figures in the English game. If he's more affable than his boss, he shares with him a disdain for those who criticise his work.

'We're hypocrites in this country, we have a national league, and a national association, and yet, we're sending our best players away all the time. But how can we say that they shouldn't go? What have we got to offer them here? I'm in the national league, very proud of being in it, and very proud that we're trying to put structures together, but saying that, you have to be realistic and say, "We don't have anything here." Give me something so that I can say to a kid, honourably, "You'd be better off staying here with Bray than going across to England." If I did that now, I'd be depriving him of the chance of a lifetime.'

After 14 years in the game, Devlin remains utterly enthralled by his job. The success of Damien Duff has fuelled his determination to create a new Irish dimension at Newcastle over the coming years. Familiarity with the operation hasn't stolen any of its romance. Devlin remains as besotted by the talent-spotting as he has always been with the game itself.

'If I could sum up scouting for you, it's like you walking into a nightclub and finding the girl of your dreams. She could be a nice-looking girl, with a wonderful personality, but the first time you know she's the one is when it hits you here in the gut. When I walk onto a football pitch, it's the same thing. The first practical things that I'm looking for are skill, temperament and pace but my gut feeling will tell me the rest. At the end of it all, something happens that I connect to, and I think that this lad has a chance. Then I watch him a couple of times and like with a girlfriend, you build up a relationship and you think, it's time to get married, and that's exactly what you do.'

Chapter Four

Teach the young and they will prosper

I The history

When Don Seery's football burst one Friday evening in 1928, he and his pals on Richmond Road had trouble rustling up the 17 shillings and six pence needed to fund the purchase of a replacement. Without a proper football, their participation in the local street league was in doubt. So, swallowing their pride, they went around the corner to Home Farm Road. They knocked on the door of number 31 and asked Brendan Menton if they could throw their lot in with his team. After Menton said yes, they divvied up the officerships between them. Seery became treasurer and Menton took the title of secretary, positions they would occupy for half a century and more.

Unwittingly, these boys in their early teens, on an estate in the northside of Dublin city, had just given birth to an institution. In time, the name of the team was abbreviated to plain Home Farm, and they outgrew the local street league to become the most fabled schoolboy club in Ireland, their name inextricably linked with some of Ireland's finest ever players, from Johnny Carey and Liam Whelan in one era, through to Ronnie Whelan and Gary Kelly in another. Nearly

50 Home Farm alumni have won senior international caps and when Ireland played the Czech Republic in March, 1998, six of the players used by Mick McCarthy had been schooled in their Whitehall headquarters.

The first home of the club that now boasts pitches at six venues across Dublin, and a reputation promulgated by the likes of Sir Matt Busby and Bob Paisley, amongst others, was a modest tract of church land known as 'The Thatch'. Before that, substitutes used to double-job as look-outs for fear that irate landowners might discover the games and hunt them from their fields. As he chuckles at the memory of clambering over ditches with farmers in hot pursuit, Brendan Menton's eyes light up. If the passing years have thieved some of the sprightliness from his step, he is still a very lively eighty-something.

Five years after finally stepping down as club secretary, he is still knee-deep in work. He juggles his post as honorary secretary of the business representatives' body, IBEC, with running a vice-presidents' committee in Home Farm and his latest task of compiling the club history. When Don Seery died on Palm Sunday in 1991, Menton decided that some sort of tribute was due to his friend. Taking into account that he was now the last suriving founding member, he began putting their story to paper.

'It's not an easy project at all. Back in those early days, we were all doers. We had no time for keeping records or minutes of meetings and discussions. We were too busy trying to expand our teams at all times to ever think of stopping to write something down.'

The living-room of Menton's house is a museum to a life spent in the service of the game. On the wall above the fireplace, a framed memento of his People of the Year award is jockeying for position with a Home Farm clock. The coffee table creaks under the weight of an enormous chunk of Waterford Crystal that has Menton's face etched into one side, a present from his club. In another corner, another piece of glass bears the familiar Liver bird logo, a gift from Liverpool FC.

Menton speaks with the assured tone of a man whose day

job for many years was advising successive governments on economic policy. The fact that in his spare time, he breathed the same air as boys who became giants just made his life all the fuller. 'I remember Johnny Carey coming all the way over from Baggott Street on the southside to train with us. Johnny was an unbelievable player. A funny thing though is that Manchester United played him at inside left for five years before Matt Busby made him into a defender. We knew all along that defence was his best position because he'd starred there for us. Johnny's reputation was such that he became known in England as "Gentleman Johnny".'

Strictly Catholic and teetotal, Johnny Carey was an intelligent, moral individual whose leadership qualities led Busby to make him United captain at a time when some still cast doubt on his playing ability. Carey embodied all that Menton and his peers wished Home Farm to be associated with because the club always took as much pride in their players' attitudes off the field as in their achievements on it. In the early years, many of their teams were peopled by acolytes of Corpus Christi, and from the start, the club sought to cultivate their own private grounds because they felt this would make it easier to maintain proper standards of behaviour.

Liam Whelan, another whom Home Farm gave to Manchester United perhaps best exemplified the virtues they wished to inculcate. 'Years ago, Bobby Charlton wrote in his book that he always wanted to become the best footballer in Britain but he felt that he could never be as good as Liam was. Liam was an extraordinary fella and a very religious man too. I can still picture the spot up in Whitehall where I said goodbye to him. He was working in Cassidy's in George's Street at the time, and we were sorry to see him go but we knew he was good enough to make it. I just shook his hand and said "Godspeed".'

To spend a couple of hours in the company of Brendan Menton is to shuffle relentlessly between generations. A minute or two on how the merits of Everton centre-half Richard Dunne were apparent at an early age can diverge into a vivid recollection of a dinner with the Busby Babes in a Dublin restaurant before merging into dissertations on old Home Farm youth teams, backboned by the likes of Amby Fogarty, Liam Whelan and the newspaper tycoon, Tony O'Reilly.

'Tony O'Reilly was an excellent centre-forward for us. He was good enough to get a schoolboy trial with Ireland once but he couldn't make it, he had a rugby match fixed for the same time.'

Menton never played rugby himself but Home Farm did dabble in other sports. For a time, in the 1930s, they fielded hurling teams until eventually, the logistics of circumventing the GAA's ban on foreign games proved too much and one code had to go. Athletics was another branch of the club that flourished for a time, and even volleyball and baseball teams have lined out in the Home Farm colours through the decades. In the end though, none of them could hold the interest of the youngsters like soccer.

As he trawls through the years, Menton's memory is jogged every now and again by a lucid reminiscence. 'Our first set of jerseys were these awful blue and brown hooped things that must have been a job lot from somewhere. After a year, we got another nicer set of blue and white hoops and we stuck with them. Then, a local businessman called Charlie Ridgeway helped us come up with a crest of a man sowing seeds in a field. It was appropriate all right because we were firm believers in "*Mol an oige agus tiocfaidh siad*" – teach the young and they will prosper.'

The motto that informed the club's thinking also seems to have been a trademark of Menton's own life. Having joined the civil service after school, he happened upon a career in economics. 'I was going past Eason's in O'Connell Street one time, and I had a few shillings in my pocket. This book caught my eye. It was called *Nature and the Significance of Economic Phenomena*. I went in and bought it and read it from cover to cover and I think from that moment on, I wanted to become an economist.'

Once Menton had gained formal qualifications as an external student from the London School of Economics, he married a woman called Anna Duff and settled in Clontarf.

Soon after that, TK Whitaker brought him into the Department of Finance where he stayed until moving to AIB in the early 1970s. As his career curved ever upwards so too did the fortunes of his club.

In 1962, Menton and Don Seery began a campaign to gain membership of the League of Ireland. It seemed like the next logical step for such a successful schoolboy nursery but for ten consecutive years, they were rebuffed by officialdom. At one stage, the club began playing friendlies against clubs from Northern Ireland to demonstrate their worth and bolster their cause. 'After one game against Glentoran, there was a report in the *Evening Herald* saying that the knocking on the door of King Lear was nothing compared to the sound of Home Farm knocking on the door of the League of Ireland. In 1972, they finally relented and let us in.'

The club's FAI cup victory just three years after their admission is perhaps Menton's favourite moment in the club's history. Then, in another breath, he mentions as equally heart-warming a day a couple of years back when he attended a game between Shamrock Rovers and Dundalk at the RDS in Dublin. That afternoon, both the managers and 15 of the players on duty had come through the ranks at Home Farm. For Menton, that was just one more measurement of their impact.

'A man called Leo Fitzmaurice started the street leagues in our area to compensate for the lack of a proper green belt. And once we set up the club, we were lucky in that local businessmen approved of what we were doing and backed us. There was no great altruism involved on our part, we just wanted a football club, somewhere for kids like us to play.'

II The legend

As the British European Airways twin-engine Elizabethan RMA readied itself for a third attempt to take off from Munich airport, it was Johnny Berry who articulated the fears that up to then had remained largely unspoken among the Manchester United team. Berry, a fearless winger by reputation, offered the opinion that the way things were looking, they would all die here on this German airstrip. Liam Whelan, the most religious man on the team, remained stoic at the suggestion. 'If that's going to happen, I'm ready for it. I hope we all are.'

Christy Whelan had been on picket duty. Dublin Corporation were on strike during the winter of 1958, and Christy had spent his day walking the line with his friends, Dazzer Keogh and Lukey Flaherty. By the time he got back to his mother's house in Cabra, he needed warming up. He sat himself down in the armchair by the fire, and waited for the heat to kick in. Out the back, in the extension they had built on, his mother was doing the ironing.

It was around tea-time when Charlie Jackson knocked on the door. Charlie used to run teams in Home Farm, and was a friend of the family. The first thing Christy noticed was the startled look on Charlie's face. When Mrs Elizabeth Whelan came in from the back to greet the visitor, she stopped in her tracks. Seeing that Charlie was still in his Guinness overalls, she sensed something was amiss.

Standing in the doorway, she asked him what was wrong. 'The plane's after crashing,' he said. She shook her head, saying: 'No, they're home Charlie, they're home by now.' All the while, she was pointing to the clock on the dresser. Liam Whelan always kept his mother informed of his movements, and she knew exactly what time the plane carrying Manchester United back from Belgrade had been due in Ringway Airport. Charlie said nothing. He just shook his head.

The blazer was a badge of honour then. The difference between those who had made it and those who hoped to. After 14 first team appearances, Matt Busby would send a player to the tailors for a fitting, and in doing so, announce in this way that he had arrived. Thumbing through the back issues of the *Manchester Evening News* from that period, the clothes they wear in the photographs allow the reader to chart the development of the younger players. Those without blazers on the way up, those with blazers already there.

Liam Whelan was never too fond of the blazer. Away from Old Trafford and matchdays, he felt it was showy and gave off the wrong impression about the wearer. On those occasions when he was ordered to don it for a function, he'd drape his plastic raincoat over his left arm so that it neatly concealed the club crest that distinguished this particular blazer from every other. That was just his way.

The passage of time has only served to amplify every one of Liam Whelan's virtues. He was quiet; so much so that Busby himself expressed concerns that his reserved nature might hold him back. He was religious; to the extent that in the build-up to the 1957 FA Cup final, a crazy rumour went around that he was intent on going off to become a priest. He was modest; watching a match up in Dalymount Park one time, he left early because he felt his presence was attracting too much attention and detracting from the game.

'For a footballer, he was unique in that he was a non-swearer,' says Wilf McGuinness. 'He was so religious that the worst thing I ever heard him say was "Damn" and that was during a reserve team match against Stoke. The funny thing was that he was booked for that. We used to joke that he should have become a priest because he was already a saint.'

The priest story gained credence after Liam posed in the clerical outfit of a friend, Father Mulholland, for a jape. 'He was religious, but all our family were,' says Christy. 'Nobby Stiles told me a story once about how Liam had heard him say the F word during a game of table tennis after training. Nobby said that at the time, he'd have preferred if the Pope had caught him instead of Liam.'

Liam Whelan's blazer now hangs proudly in the new, extended Manchester United museum. Forty years after its owner perished in the Munich air crash at the age of 22, the famous crest he fretted over stares out at passers-by. Not a plastic raincoat in sight.

The four years that separated him from his younger brother

allowed Christy Whelan sufficient distance to properly appreciate Liam's talents. From when he saw him in playground games with a team called the Red Rockets, he sensed he was something special. Bulwarked by Liam and his friend, Ronnie Whelan senior (no relation but father of the former Liverpool star), the Rockets toured the playgrounds of Dublin taking on all comers. From Mountjoy Square to Broadstone and even as far south as Ringsend, they remained unbeaten for two years.

In time, the Red Rockets gave way to the more organised games of Home Farm. Nobody still in the club remembers exactly how Liam Whelan signed up, they are just glad that he did. Christy Whelan continued to monitor his brother's progress zealously. One particular season, when Liam's Home Farm team played all their games on a Sunday, Christy and his brother-in-law Michael actually switched clubs so that their own fixtures fell on Saturdays. If Liam was playing, they felt it was worth being there.

'I used to come home to my mother, and say "Ma, I can't understand how no club have come in for Liam. He's the best player I've ever seen in Dublin." My mother used to say: "Are you sure, that's not just because you're his brother?" But I was proved right. Two months after he left Dublin for United, there was a Brazilian club offering £100,000 for him.'

In the Spring of 1953, Manchester United were casting around desperately for a player to bolster their team for the forthcoming FA Youth Cup final against Wolves. An injury to John Doherty, an influential member of the team, had hastened their quest for new talent. Matt Busby despatched Bert Whalley to Dublin, armed with the name of Vinny Ryan, a prolific goalscorer with Home Farm.

Billy Behan, the scout responsible for sending Johnny Carey, John Giles, Tony Dunne and Paul McGrath to Old Trafford, persuaded Whalley that Whelan was a better bet. Thirty years later, in Eamon Dunphy's book, *A Strange Kind of Glory* Behan explained the transfer saga. 'He (Whalley) had been sent with this name, and I said "Look, take Liam, he'll do the job for you." But Bert went back to consult Jimmy Murphy (Matt Busby's assistant) – I think he was afraid of Jimmy – in the end, they got in touch and Liam went over.'

Liam Whelan was working in Cassidy's drapers when United came in. There was no talk of a trial, they were offering an immediate contract. Manchester United won the Youths Cup 8-2 on aggregate and Liam scored in both legs.

At that time, Johnny Carey, another Home Farm alumnus, was the Manchester United captain, and meeting the new recruit at Old Trafford one day, he asked the youngster his name. 'Liam, is it?' enquired Carey. 'Well, hold on to it for as long as you can. They're sure to take it away from you here.' Carey was right. The boy whose mother christened him William but who was called Liam soon became Billy.

Billy Whelan found Manchester difficult to settle in. He enjoyed the company of his peers, sharing digs with Bobby Charlton for two years, but he missed his family terribly. Nobody realised this more than his mother, and Mrs Whelan was inclined to take appropriate action. Twice during his time there she had operations to remove tumours, and on each occasion, she dispatched Christy to Manchester so that he would be present when Liam opened the letters telling him the news. 'I think she was afraid that if he was on his own when he got the news, he'd have jumped up and come home,' says Christy.

With his career graph on an inexorable rise, returning to Dublin was never a realistic option, and they eventually came up with a solution to combat his loneliness. Liam moved in with another Dubliner, Brendan Doran, and his family who lived in Stockport. Brendan, a brother of Christy's best friend, Sean, managed a canning factory for the Edwards family, proprietors of Manchester United. In hindsight, Christy Whelan's only regret is that Liam didn't make that move earlier.

After the crash, Christy travelled to Manchester to pick up Liam's belongings: 'He had an old Austin car that was falling apart, and I was driving along in it with Sean Doran, and this policeman stopped us. He got out his notebook and started walking around the car. He started writing, and he said: "Do you know the steering is bad? Do you know the tyres are bald?" He went through a litany of faults, and Sean said: "To tell you the truth officer, we don't know anything about the car. As a matter of fact, it's Liam Whelan's car and that's his brother there." "Oh God," the policeman said. "I'm so sorry, I wouldn't do anything on Liam, he was too good."'

Some said he was too slow yet more often than not, he finished first in the one-mile races they had in training. Others reckoned his mild demeanour might militate against his future development, but this is the man who went to see Matt Busby shortly before Munich to ask why he was out of the side. There was talk as well that he was too slight, although Wilf McGuinness maintains that 'when you hit him in training, you stayed hit.'

Playing inside right, Whelan scored 28 First Division goals as Manchester United won their second consecutive title in 1956/57. Their attempt to win the Double that season was thwarted by Aston Villa in the FA Cup final but even that day Whelan added lustre to his reputation. When United's keeper Ray Wood was taken off injured, he was replaced in goal by Jackie Blanchflower, and Whelan moved back to right half, where, one contemporary observer noted: 'He played a game that staggered even his most fervent admirers.'

In an Irish career of only four caps, the drawn game against England at Dalymount Park in May 1957 left one abiding memory. Before the match, his Manchester United team-mate, the legendary Duncan Edwards, had warned Whelan against performing his trademark nutmegging routine. After Whelan nutmegged Edwards for the second time that day, the English star tapped him on the ankle and the home crowd booed and hissed.

There is no doubt that a premature and tragic death can often colour people's judgements. More than one average sportsperson has undergone posthumous and undeserved apotheosis. Liam Whelan's career statistics are 96 appearances, 52 goals, two league medals. In this context, perhaps the most telling evaluation of his true worth was

Busby's pre-Munich assertion that he envisaged Bobby Charlton and Whelan becoming his Puskas and Di Stefano.

Ironic then that in the reshuffle that preceded Christmas 1957, it was Charlton who replaced Whelan as Busby dropped four of his Babes before the team embarked on an unbeaten run that was to stretch as far as their match in Belgrade against Red Star. Their last game together. 'When I got into the side that time, it was at Liam's expense,' said Bobby Charlton once. 'But he would have been back because he was such a dedicated professional.'

Christy Whelan learned the worst in a phone call from the *Irish Independent*, the newspaper which had been the family's chief source of information since Charlie Jackson first called. Christy took the call in Mrs Farrell's house up the street as the Whelans had no phone themselves. The rest of that night passed in a haze of visitors. Home Farm people, football folk, family, friends, neighbours: all calling to offer condolences and help. Christy Whelan spent the evening shuttling between the telephone in Mrs Farrell's and the packed family home.

Later on, somebody suggested that everybody should leave so that the Whelans could get some rest. When they went upstairs, Mrs Whelan called out to her son: 'If it was true about Liam, Christy, the guards would have to call to tell us.'

Christy replied: 'Did you not hear them, Ma? They came when you were in the sitting-room?'

III The creed – past

Joe Fitzpatrick leans out of his chair, picks up an immaculately-kept photo album and begins reeling in the years. Between 1949 and 1985, Joe coached teams in Home Farm to win 39 trophies. 'I suppose it wasn't too bad a record,' he says now. The bald statistics tell only half the story, the photo album eloquently portrays the rest. Between its covers is a pictorial history that spans the ages, from sepia prints to technicolour, from post-war crewcuts through the hirsute '70s into the naff '80s, all the while reminding one of the different generations this man has straddled.

As he flips to and fro between decades, the names trip easily from his tongue. 'There's Paddy Mulligan, he started with me, a very good player him. He played for West Brom and Chelsea after.' Another photograph, and another youthful face stirs his mind. 'Joe Haverty, he went to Arsenal, he played with me too . . . Joe Carolan, he was at Manchester United . . . oh, and there's Ronnie Whelan, he was one of mine too.' In between name-checking all the famous graduates, he dawdles over one particular picture and points out a tousle-haired, smiling youngster. 'See that boy there, he would have been a very famous player but he was killed by a bus when he was 13. That was the worst time I ever remember in football.'

Joe Fitzpatrick came late to Home Farm. A southsider by birth, he played most of his career in junior football with Rossville. At 26, he signed for Home Farm, and within three years, they gave him a team to manage. 'There was a committee up there, a schoolboy committee, and you had to be asked. A fella called Tom Smith, he saw me playing for the first team, and he asked would I like to run a team. I thought that I knew a lot about football because I read a lot about it, and I played a lot and I could have gone to England if I wanted to. But this fellow, Tom Smith, he used to give coaching classes and when I went to those, I began to see that there was a lot in football that I didn't know. Smith had a great system, and it's funny you should be asking me this now but it was based on the old Arsenal system.

'There was a manager there called Herbert Chapman who won the English First Division three times with Huddersfield, and he would have won it three times with Arsenal only he died halfway through the last season. We based our defensive systems on Chapman, the double centre-halves. Football was much different then than it is now. At the time there was no coaching and Chapman was one of the first I knew of to actually coach.

'To give you an idea, I was looking at a documentary on

the telly recently about football in the past. I think it was either Nat Lofthouse or Tommy Lawton who was picked by Alf Ramsey in the early '60s, and they were complaining that Ramsey was coaching the players, telling them what to do. I'd been doing that with Tom Smith in Home Farm for over ten years before that. That'll tell you the difference between Home Farm and the rest. Every team in the club followed the same Chapman system, and if somebody heard you were playing a different way, you were in trouble. I have no doubt that Tom Smith was way before his time in his ideas.'

Fitzpatrick had a thirst for knowledge of the game which wasn't sated even by Smith's revolutionary ideas. Having become a fan of the German method of playing the game, he sent off to that country seeking some of their training manuals. 'I knew from reading all the German books that the key to the whole thing was ball control and I knew you had to practise to attain that sort of thing. I believed completely in ball skills but the trouble back then was figuring out where you were going to get the footballs from. With Home Farm, you were given one ball per team at the start of the season, and if you wanted any more, you had to buy them yourself. I did too, although not that often.'

At the age of 78, Fitzpatrick remains obsessed by football. Watching a live Premiership match in the Home Farm clubhouse recently, he fell off a stool while attempting, unconsciously, to kick a ball. Telling the story inspires a memory of a similar incident from years back. 'I used to get so involved in games, I was living every moment of every game. Playing St Kevin's up in Whitehall once, our goalkeeper dived to make a save and I dived too. I found myself sprawled out in the mud. That's nothing to boast about, I suppose.'

His devotion to the cause never inured Fitzpatrick to the downside of the game. As Home Farm's success grew, their name became a magnet for budding footballers of all abilities. With the pick of the crop available to them back then, it fell to the manager to make the cuts in his squad. 'Every year we'd have trials, and tonnes and tonnes of kids would come up and you felt like an executioner at times

Halifax Town's Kieran O'Regan, playing for Ireland against Poland in a friendly at Dalymount Park in 1984 (© INPHO/Billy Stickland)

Shay Given: his father, Seamus, predicted Shay would play for Ireland before he was 21 – and he did (© INPHO/Billy Stickland)

Dave Langan, in happier times and familiar pose, playing for Ireland against Belgium in a World Cup qualifier in Brussels (© INPHO/Billy Stickland)

Pat Devlin, manager of Brae Wanderers and scout for Newcastle United: 'You don't have to be Einstein to know where the best players are playing' (© INPHO/Matt Browne)

John Freeman at his school of excellence for young players in Offaly, where talented soccer players are nurtured in the heart of hurling country (© INPHO)

TOP AND ABOVE: Home Farm: it took a vociferous ten-year campaign, led by Brendan Menton and Don Seery, before the club finally gained their rightful place in the National League of Ireland(© INPHO/Tom Honan/Matt Browne)

LEFT: David Warren, Desmond Byrne and Keith Foy celebrate Ireland's first major championship victory at any level following the Under-16s' European Championship final against Italy (© INPHO/Lorraine O'Sullivan)

RIGHT: Captain Shaun Byrne shares the plaudits with team manager Brian Kerr and coach Noel O'Reilly on that famous day in Perth, Scotland (© INPHO/Lorraine O'Sullivan)

ABOVE: Home-coming: David Warren holds the trophy aloft as the victors parade the spoils through the city (© INPHO/Lorraine O'Sullivan)

TOP: Victorious again: Brian Kerr salutes the travelling support in Cyprus after his Under-18 team beat Germany in another European final
(© INPHO/Lorraine O'Sullivan)
BOTTOM: The Under-16 team that will go down in history
(© INPHO/Lorraine O'Sullivan)

ABOVE LEFT AND RIGHT: St Patrick's Athletic's Pat Dolan, the football evangelist striving to bring his club and the National League to a higher level (©INPHO/Billy Stickland)

BELOW: One of Dolan's signings Leon Braithwaite celebrates another St Pat's goal (© INPHO/Lorraine O'Sullivan)

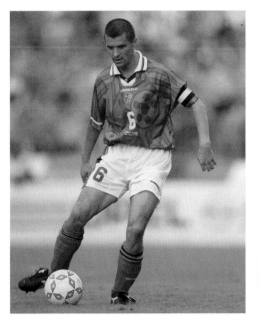

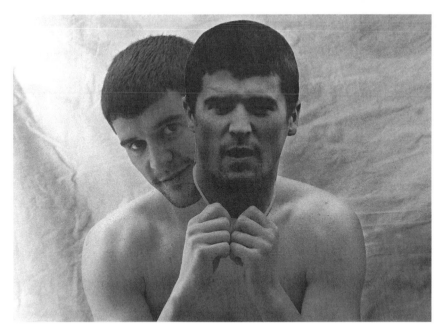

Roy Keane: the Manchester United and Ireland captain at
work, rest and play
(© INPHO/Keith Heneghan/Lorraine O'Sullivan/Billy Stickland)

Maire Rua Gallagher: back home in Donegal, but still supporting Celtic more than 50 years after her first Old Firm game (© INPHO/Patrick Bolger)

having to cut them off. At the end, you'd bring them into this room and it was called the execution chamber. One particular day, two players came in and I had to choose one of them. I signed one because I thought he looked more like a footballer than the other fella. The guy I picked was Paddy Brady, Liam's brother. He went on to play for Ireland and for a couple of teams in England after.

'I probably got lucky like that a few times because I was fairly successful, winning 39 trophies and all. I think it was about 12 senior internationals started their football with me, Ken Cunningham was the last. He came to me in 1985, shortly before I retired.' With that, he re-opens the book, and points out a cheeky-grinned Cunningham smiling out of one more team photograph, one more silent testament to Fitzpatrick's own ability.

IV The creed – present

There are few, if any, schoolboy clubs in the world which can boast a full-time director of coaching with the pedigree of Liam Tuohy. His playing CV is decorated with domestic honours, a spell with Newcastle United and international caps. That's an impressive enough read until compared with his managerial equivalent: in charge of a Shamrock Rovers team which won six consecutive FAI Cups, the manager of the Irish senior team at a time when they turned the corner from mediocrity towards respectability, and the coaching genius who qualified Irish youth teams for three European championships and a World Cup in the '80s.

Tuohy is not of Home Farm stock. Growing up in East Wall in Dublin, he played for a team called St Mary's who mockingly used refer to Home Farm teams as 'the altar boys'. 'Home Farm were the best team in my schoolboy days and we resented them deeply. They were the best turned out, they'd be all kitted out perfectly and we were like street urchins next to them. In those days, most of the other teams didn't train or were lucky to get full teams out if they did. Home Farm were better organised, they seemed to be physically stronger and they'd normally be winning matches very easily.'

When Home Farm invited Tuohy on board in 1989, he was running a travelling coaching school that brought his gospel to all corners of the country, and the satisfaction that job was bringing him made the call from Whitehall timely. 'They had nobody supervising the coaching here and I took the job because it was something that I wanted to be involved in. I had become disenchanted with the whole management thing. I'd been there, done that, but I was really enjoying the coaching end, and this was a chance for me to get involved with kids again.'

For decades, one of the cornerstones of Home Farm's success was a system of mini-leagues which allowed young boys their first access to the club. At the end of the competition, the most talented individuals would then be invited to join a Home Farm team proper. Over time, the officials discovered that many youngsters were participating in the leagues even though they had already committed themselves to a different team. This meant that though they were benefiting from the Home Farm structures, the club was ultimately losing out on them. A new scheme was required.

'Every Saturday morning, we run an induction course into the club for six-, seven- and eight-year-olds. We have between 50 and 60 boys coming in every weekend for a two-hour coaching session. The way we operate is that there are five different coaches and we split them up so that we have passing there, heading there, shooting there, dribbling there, and a match there, and we rotate them every 20 minutes because if you were to leave any boy without a match, you wouldn't be able to live with yourself. Kids of that age aren't capable of taking on board anything except technique.

'The first thing a six-year-old does when he gets the ball is that he runs with it until somebody takes it off him but when you work with him, he eventually takes on board the passing element of it. The hardest thing of all is asking them to stop being everywhere the ball is. Once we get them out of that, we show them how to make turns with a ball. There are four or five basic turns with a ball in the game, and we would show them how to make those. That would be based on the Ajax method and outside of that, it's pretty basic stuff. In their early teens, when it becomes necessary, we make them aware of tactics and the need to press.'

Each weekend, 18 schoolboy teams take to the fields of Dublin wearing the blue and white of Home Farm. Many of the players will be following in the footsteps of fathers and even grandfathers. Over time, the club has become a birthright and the same surnames backbone teams across the decades. Just as Ronnie Whelan's father played for the club before him, so now too do his nephews after him. In this way, the bloodlines running through the club history are flawless.

Every single outfit has a manager, a coach and a third person looking after them. The pool of mentors is a mixture of former League of Ireland players, qualified coaches and willing parents. Getting the quality of people who are suited for the job can be difficult, but that they evidently succeed in doing so is borne out by the fact that in the season 1996/97, Home Farm won national competitions at Under-12, -13, -14 and -15 levels. There are other barometers too. One recent team, managed by Paddy Hillard, went through from Under-9s to Under-18s unbeaten and, in so doing, gained an entry in the *Guinness Book of Records*. If much has changed since the time of Joe Fitzpatrick and Tom Smith, the pursuit of excellence remains the same.

'I don't know whether it was policy or not but there was a time here when they always played a sweeper. That was still in vogue when I came and I changed that. I don't have anything against the sweeper but if you're playing one style right through the club, you're ignoring the fact that one team might be better at playing a certain style of football than another. I mean if you have Brazil, you're not going to ask them to play like Wimbledon, and if you have Wimbledon, you're not going to ask them to play like Brazil. If a side needs a sweeper they should have one, but that doesn't mean you have to play 18 sweepers.

'Every team should play to their strengths, to whatever the sum total of their talents is. What we're about now is producing skilful ball-players who can go out and play well and win games. If one is being honest though, the players and mentors at Home Farm want to win badly enough that they know there are times when a long ball is vital. What I will say though is that if you have a young kid, you're not going to bring him up playing that way, you're going to try and bring him up as a footballer.

'And when you're trying to develop boys, if you see their weakness it's in your own interest to sort it out. If he's not good in the air, that should come into part of his coaching, if he's very one-footed you try and sort that out. Either you work on the weak foot or you teach him how to always turn the ball onto his strong foot. I'm not suggesting we're perfect by any means but we've a lot of good people running our teams and that shows.'

The exact definition of Tuohy's role is as an overseer of all teams. He takes each side for a couple of specialised sessions every season while being available to advise all coaches if they want him to. When a Home Farm team is going to represent the club abroad, which almost every side does at some stage, he works extensively with them in the months preceding their trip, preparing them to measure themselves against the very best schoolboy teams.

'Before our boys go to something like the Milk Cup, I would do some stuff with them. They are going to be playing against the very best opposition in Europe, and I'd just be trying to get them to move the ball that bit quicker. The only essential difference in football is that the good teams move the ball quicker than the bad teams. They have the technique to control the ball and pass it quicker. We try to give the boys the chance to play against the best teams we can, but don't think we haven't got plenty of good clubs up against us in Dublin. We're not the only club in this city that are striving for excellence.'

That such a high percentage of Home Farm players are making it in England and into the international team does seem to indicate that somehow this club is making a better fist of it than most. Tuohy is all in favour of these youngsters making a bid for glory in the Premiership and would even like it if some of the more talented teenagers were being courted by European clubs.

'When I was managing the Irish team (1971-73), I found it difficult to pick a team which didn't have a League of Ireland player in it because we didn't have the quantity or quality of players based in England then. We're certainly getting the quantity now, and I think we're getting the quality too. Look at Stephen McPhail at Leeds, he played all his career here. He has a left foot that is perfection, one of those guys who was composed on the ball even if he was surrounded by people and a great passer. His emergence at Elland Road will be satisfying for everybody here.

'Nothing changes in football anyway. Defenders still defend, attackers still attack. I wouldn't like it to appear that I've revolutionised anything. This crowd have won trophies and produced great players long before I came along, and probably will continue to do so after I'm gone. See all those winning pennants, they speak for themselves.' As he speaks, Tuohy is pointing at an array of blue and white pennants commemorating each league or cup victory in every age group which stretches all along the wall, one more vivid reflection of the ethos.

In the centre of the clubhouse bar, there's an enormous wooden plaque on which the names of every Home Farm player who has represented Ireland at senior level is etched. This particular afternoon in April, Tuohy remarks that the names of Alan Maybury, Mark Kinsella and Graham Kavanagh, the very latest caps, are waiting to be inscribed. On other walls, there is a colourful collection of pennants, the gifts of clubs which Home Farm have competed against or entertained. The names speak for themselves. Celtic, Manchester United, Leeds United, Ajax. Hallowed names indeed, Home Farm doesn't look out of place in their company.

Chapter Five

The sad ballad
of Davy Langan

He has thought seriously about selling his medals, plundering the cabinet of his parents' house, where they form the centre-piece of a display that chronicles his career, and cashing in his chips. A man who played 26 times for his country has been reduced to that. Two weeks ago, he broached the idea with an old friend who dissuaded him from the notion, telling him he would never forgive himself later. When he asked his mother what she thought, her only response was to break down in tears, saying 'Please, don't.' A 15-year professional career yielded Milk Cup honours and a Second Division championship. Not a bad return, but life after football has given Davy Langan more pressing concerns than the sanctity of some metal mementos of past glories.

He is 41 now, and officially registered as disabled. He works as a porter in Peterborough town hall because under the positive discrimination law, 3 per cent of council employees must be from the ranks of the disabled. If the pay is hard on the pocket, the job is at least easy on his ravaged body. There is no heavy lifting to hurt his back problem and the most onerous task he performs is to set out the teas and coffees in the council chamber. Invariably, some of the people he meets are kinder than others. His career with

Peterborough, his sixth and final club, was brief but there's always someone there to remind him how far he's fallen.

'The council is a big place, and when some people find out that I was an ex-professional footballer, they will make snide comments like: "Oh, you've come down to earth with a bang mate, haven't you?" They do say some nasty things but you get used to it because you have to. No matter how nasty the things they say, you have to just bite your tongue and carry on. I have to walk away.'

He has to walk away because fighting would be beneath and beyond him. His left knee is in such a dreadful state that every two years for the rest of his life, he will require an operation to clean out the mounting detritus of wear and tear. His back condition requires him to use a specially adapted chair at work, and means that frequently, he sleeps more comfortably on the hard lounge room floor than he does in his bed. He takes pain-killing medication every morning and some days it dulls the pain more than others, but in any case, it doesn't help his movement any.

For the professional athlete, the inertia is a handicap in itself. Langan loved the lifestyle of the professional footballer, replete with its age-old mantra of train and sleep. Even when he'd come back to Dublin for the close-season, he could never rest. Morning and evening, he'd be out running. An hour's jog along Sandymount Strand followed by a half-hour of muscle exercises. Everybody was always telling him to slow down but for him, there was nothing like the feeling of a body in tune with itself.

His movement is so restricted now that he cannot manage a brisk walk. The only sop he can make to physical fitness is swimming three times a week, and even that must be done at a certain pace. His metabolism has ensured that he hasn't piled on the pounds like some retired footballers do but his face is fuller than it used to be. In any case, the weight issue is only a sideline. In his position, vanity about personal appearance has long given way to more serious concerns about the way his injuries impact upon his everyday life.

He knelt down to mend a bike puncture once and found

that he couldn't get back up, as straightening the knees out again was too painful. The embarrassment he felt only made the pain seem worse. When there's a job that needs doing around the house, something as simple and mundane as changing a lightbulb, his wife Debbie or her father has to do it. It hurts him to see it but he knows there's no other way. These are all debilitating on the spirit but that he is forever denied even the simple pleasure of kicking a ball around his back garden with his nine-year-old son, Calum, is perhaps the worst.

'It kills me that I can't run around with the kids. Calum supports Manchester United and is football mad. All I can do is roll him a football and get him to kick it back to me but I can't do anything else. I feel sorry for my little boy. He wants to run around playing football all the time like I did with my Da years ago, but I'm just not up to it. It's the same with my little girl, Leah, who's six. If I lift her up, I have to put her straight back down again as the nerves start attacking me at the back. It's an awful way to be. I'd like a proper family life but I know that I can't have it.'

His voice throughout the conversation is depressed and downbeat. It seems strange to listen and to imagine that in the old days, the good old days, Langan was the post-international match master of ceremonies, charged with the task of getting the traditional sing-song underway. To start proceedings, he might launch into his own version of 'Molly Malone' or beseech somebody like Kevin Moran to give a few bars of 'Step It Out Mary.'

It is difficult to reconcile that image with this, and yet, now and again, usually when he is talking about his schoolboy days in Dublin, or his international career, his tone becomes more animated. The memories of better times seem to infuse him with hope and in the cold, harsh reality of his present predicament, the thoughts of what he used to be sometimes serve to make him feel warm again. Sometimes.

Lansdowne Road used to love Davy Langan. He grew up a corner kick from the ground, and when he got the ball, he invariably attacked the right flank. Nominally a full-back, it was his unorthodox wing play that the crowd acclaimed. The ball would come to him on or around halfway and he'd set off. As soon as he'd cross the border into the opposing half, it always seemed like there was somebody in the background turning up the volume button on the cheers. The noise was intoxicating and it made him feel invincible. When a journalist interviewed him after his international début, he remarked: 'I can die happy now, I've played for my country.' The passage of two decades hasn't dimmed the romance.

'Playing for Ireland was always fantastic for me. When you walked out at Lansdowne, and I'm sure it was like this for the rest of the players, you'd think you'd died and gone to heaven. You walked out and that crowd, the roar would go up, and you're wearing your shirt and it's so, so loud. The crowd would roar when I'd go down the wing, and it made me feel ten foot tall, like I could beat anybody. I loved that, I miss that terrible, I miss it something awful, it's such a short career, and it goes so fast.'

When Ireland took on France in a World Cup qualifier on 14 October 1981, the Lansdowne crowd were in especially vociferous mood. Fifty-four thousand people had been shoehorned into the old ground to watch a game which Ireland needed to win to keep their slim hopes of reaching Spain alive. One particularly passionate Irish fan even had the wherewithal to steal the French tricolour from its flagpole. History would remember the Irish team which played that day as a side who were only denied qualification to the 1982 World Cup, officially by superior French goal difference, unofficially by some highly questionable refereeing during an earlier 1-0 defeat by Belgium.

The day itself was memorable as Ireland edged a 3-2 victory over a Michel Platini-inspired French team who would eventually be good enough to reach the World Cup semi-finals. It was a glorious victory, and though France went through, thanks to wins in their two remaining games, that Irish team has always held a special place in the hearts of those whose passion for the cause predated the glory years of the Charlton era.

Against France that day, Davy Langan was starting his 12th successive game for Ireland. Twenty-four years old and with a burgeoning reputation in a very good Birmingham City team, he was approaching the prime of his football life. Over the previous 18 months, he had become a fixture in the international side and all was well with his world. Unfortunately, he was about to discover that football careers, like no other profession, hinge on the smallest details. A fortuitous drop of the ball can make a champ out of a chump and one lucky break is often the only barrier between anonymity and fame, and this also works in reverse. That afternoon at Lansdowne may have become part of folklore but for Langan, it was the beginning of a nightmare.

'I remember that I tackled this fella in midfield and just when I was standing up, the ball was still loose by my feet so I flicked it away. Then the French fella came in very late and hit me on my left leg, my standing leg. My knee was wrenched back and it swelled up like a balloon. At half-time, Mick Byrne put some painkiller on it and like a fool, I played on. Playing for your country, you're so proud that you have to play on but the knee was never right again.'

Pain is relative to the surroundings a person is in. When Langan got hurt at Lansdowne Road, it didn't feel the same as it did elsewhere. With the green jersey on him, the crest of three shamrocks over his heart, and adrenalin surging through his body, he wouldn't have seen any option but to continue. The leg was sore all right, but once Mick Byrne attempted to anaesthetise it, he went back into battle like any good patriot. His family and friends were in that crowd and the local boy wasn't going to let his people down. On such brave and foolhardy decisions, a person's whole life can turn.

The morning after the game, he could barely walk. When he got back to Birmingham City, the club were furious that he had played on with the injury. Rest and a series of injections were the first prescription and within six weeks he had made a comeback of sorts. He struggled through to the end of that season, thinking a summer's recuperation would do the trick. That was only a short-term solution however, and no sooner had the next campaign begun than the leg was swelling up, and he was breaking down again. It would be two-and-a-half years before he made a proper return to the game.

'The cartilage was taken out but the worst thing was that I had an ulcer the size of a 50 pence piece that was rotting away the bones at the side of my knee. All the bones were so rotten that they had to drill the ulcer out of my knee. Then they had to take a piece of bone marrow off my hip and put it into the knee joint so the bone would grow back. I began to think that I'd never get right with that knee because they'd inject me with cortisone, and give me operation after operation.

'I regret getting the injections now because I later found out that though a cortisone injection every now and again doesn't do much damage, the amount that I had wrecked the joint inside. The last operation that I had last year, the surgeon said that the knee was in an awful mess because of all the cortisone. It was in such an awful way that he said that I'll end up having a plastic knee joint.'

Rehabilitating athletes inevitably suffer another injury in recovery by putting too much pressure on an over-employed joint, and Langan was no exception. 'When I was on the crutches, they made me do body exercises in the gym to try and keep my upper half in shape, so I came up to twist one day, and I just got a sharp pain in the base of the spine. I came back down onto the concrete, and the pain was unbelievable. I'd cracked my vertebrae and that was another major operation. The surgeon did a spinal fusion because he had to fuse the vertebrae and he had to take more bone marrow out of my other hip to do it.

'My life just became a series of operations and injections. The last operation that I had at Birmingham, the surgeon said: "This is the last time, I'll give it only one more go because you can't go on like this – you'll end up in a wheelchair if this carries on. I can't keep opening you up." It did the business for a while but the knee was never really right after. Loose bits kept breaking down into the knee.'

The injuries and operations took their toll to such an extent that after a while, he considered retiring and returning to Dublin. He was going under the knife with such regularity that his mother was constantly worried. Although knee and leg operations are part of the footballer's job, hearing that her son was having serious spinal operations was too much for Mrs Langan. Before the last, mildly successful operation at Birmingham, he'd got as far as promising his family that if that didn't work, he would come home.

Langan grew up in Ringsend, an area of Dublin's docklands where only one sport dominated the childrens' lives. 'It was a soccer mad town, we used to go over to play in Ringsend Park every chance we got. Every Sunday morning after Mass, my father used to take us over, 30 or 40 of us who lived on the same streets. He'd bring us across there and organise a match. He used to love coming over to play soccer with us. He'd bring one of those old, leather footballs. We were all only about seven or eight so they were very hard to kick. It's funny I always thought that using the heavy ball would stand me in good stead later on.'

When the time was right, Bill Langan brought his son down to try out for a properly organised team, Bath Rangers. After a stint there, he graduated to Cherry Orchard, one of the most respected schoolboy outfits in the country. Davy had been impressive enough to attract the attention of Manchester United and though their legendary scout, Billy Behan, sent him over for a trial, nothing came of it. Birmingham City were another club to take him across for a look but thought better of signing him. Later they would fork out a then club record £350,000 for his services.

John Wilkes, the manager at Cherry Orchard was also Derby County's scout in Ireland, and in the end, Davy Langan began his apprenticeship at the Baseball Ground, where he came under the influence of some of the biggest names in the game. 'Brian Clough was there for a while. He wasn't half as bad as people made out that he was. He used to get you in the dressing-room, have a look at you, then bring you down to his office. You'd walk in there expecting the worst, then he'd say: "I think you look very homesick, here's a plane ticket, you go home and see your mother and father for a couple of weeks." He knew all the knacks. He knew when you were sad and knew how to get the best out of you.'

Langan was fourteen-and-a-half when he started in England, and his tender years didn't help him cope with the loneliness of living abroad. He spent his first couple of seasons ringing home and telling his mother he wanted to come back. He wasn't the only Irish boy at Derby suffering the same fate. Reeling in the years, he lists his compeers from back then. 'Don O'Riordan was there, he's managing Galway United now. Then there was a guy called Eddie Hogan, I think he's in double-glazing, and a goalkeeper from Dublin called Tony Buckley – somebody told me that he works in the post office over there.'

For the first three years, he was on the usual apprentice wage of £7 a week. When he turned professional at 18, his money was improved to £25. At the time, he couldn't believe he was making such a huge step up in wages. At a distance of more than two decades, in an era when the average Premiership footballer's wage is a few thousand pounds a week, Langan laughs now at the difference in potential earnings. 'If somebody manages five or six years at a top club now, they're made for life. I was just born 12 years or so too early, wasn't I?'

He broke into the Derby team at 19 in fortuitous circumstances. Playing in the reserves, his form in midfield had been steady rather than spectacular until an injury crisis forced the manager Colin Murphy to reshuffle his deck. 'Murphy had only been there about three months, and he pulled me into the squad and told me that I might be sub against Leeds that Saturday. Then it lashed rain all week so the match was in doubt right up to the kick-off. At quarter to two, Murphy said: "By the way, you're playing."

'It was an unbelievable surprise and he didn't give me any time to think or get nervous which was the best thing for me. If he'd have told me the day before, I wouldn't have been able to sleep, I would have been way too worried. I can still see the Baseball Ground that day, it was just all mud, a terrible surface. Joe Jordan scored for them with two minutes to go but I got the man of the match award, and it gave me great confidence.'

Such confidence indeed that over the following four seasons, he missed a total of just four league games and within a year of his Derby début, Langan was capped for the Irish senior team against Turkey. All his dreams were coming true. As a schoolboy international, he'd become friendly with one of his teenage contemporaries, Frank Stapleton, and as each pursued their career at different ends of England, they kept in touch by letter, hoping that one day they might play senior together. Eventually they did.

At this stage, Langan's career was everything he hoped it would be; a regular with an excellent Derby team, peopled at various intervals by the likes of Colin Todd, Roy McFarland, Charlie George and Kevin Hector, his club form was such that he was staking a genuine claim for the Irish right-back slot too. When Argentina came to Dublin in May, 1980, trailing Diego Maradona as the big box office draw, Eoin Hand gave Langan the task of man-marking the player who was fast becoming the best in the world.

'It was like being in a dream that day. He was so fast, he was on a different planet to the rest of us. I got booked against him because I tried to get stuck in to him. I thought that might upset him but his balance was so fantastic, he could make you look like a fool any time he wanted to. Still, it's a good memory to have.'

Even when things started going awry at the Baseball Ground, with relegation looming in the spring of 1980, Langan's reputation was such that newly-promoted Birmingham City snapped him up. He joined a Birmingham team, bulwarked by Archie Gemmill, Alan Curbishley, Colin Todd and Frank Worthington, that was good enough to finish 13th in their first season in the top flight while reaching the quarter-finals of the League Cup. But early in the following campaign, Jim Smith was sacked as club manager, and Langan barely had time to impress his new boss Ron Saunders before suffering his knee injury at Lansdowne Road.

It is a hazard of the footballer's job that clubs often show scant regard for the injured player's feelings and emotions. Birmingham stood by Langan throughout all his operations but once his contract expired in 1984, he was released. The professional game is hallmarked by its lack of sentiment and Langan only expected as much. Fortunately, Jim Smith, then manager at Oxford United, remembered the potential that he had once bought into so expensively. Smith figured that if Langan could overcome the injuries, he could do a job at the Manor Ground.

'There's no doubt that Jim Smith was the best manager for me. When I had all those injury problems at Birmingham, he still used to ring me up. When I recovered and was trying to get to play again, he gave me a trial at Oxford. Luckily the knee only swelled up a couple of times in pre-season with Oxford, and when it did, I wouldn't be able to train for a week or two. I'd rest it, let the swelling come down and then they'd inject me again.'

His knee was never fully operational but Langan contributed massively to the most successful Oxford team ever. Smith gave him a licence to attack down the flank, and told him part of his job was to ensure that the waiting John Aldridge received a decent number of crosses in each game. Langan and his team-mates christened Aldridge 'Jimmy Greaves' for his ability to profit from these while Aldridge told anyone who'd listen that Langan was worth ten goals a season to him.

Those were good times at the Manor Ground. Robert Maxwell was club chairman, and would regularly invite the players for afternoon tea at Headington Hall. Langan remembers the splendour of the venue if not the man. 'You could sense he was a sly kind of fella. He always wanted to talk about the team and he'd be asking you which players were any good or whether you liked the manager or not. He was really abrasive about it too.

'He looked after his money too. Everyone thought that he

would be a high payer because of his high profile but he wasn't. He was tight with his money and we all found out later just why. When we won the old Second Division and got promotion, we got £800 before tax. We got to the 1986 Milk Cup final, and we won it, and people think we must have earned a fortune from that. On my mother's life, we got £1,200 a man for winning, before tax. I know that QPR who we beat in the final actually got £10,000 a man just for getting there.'

The friendship with Aldridge was to yield even greater rewards for Ireland. During a dressing-room conversation one day, Aldridge mentioned that his grandmother hailed initially from Athlone, County Westmeath. Immediately aware of just what this meant in an international context, Langan contacted the FAI with the information that they should go after Aldridge.

At that time in its evolution, the FAI was a slow-moving organisation, and it was only when Jack Charlton took over as manager early in 1986, that Aldridge, and another Oxford player Ray Houghton, became a live possibility for Ireland. The rest is history, and although Langan continued to figure in Irish squads and even in the team for a year or so after the arrival of the new pair, they were perhaps his last great contribution to the Irish cause.

When he was playing for Oxford United for that period in the mid-'80s, it appeared as if Davy Langan's career had run along the same familiar lines as all of his Irish contemporaries. Sure, it had been complicated by severe injury but otherwise he climbed the same ladder as every Irish player in England: apprentice, reserve, first team and then international. His story is unremarkable enough in many ways, except, in the modern era, there is scarcely another in the Irish game with an ending bathed in as much pathos as this.

The Irish team that played France that day was one of the strongest sides put out in the pre-Charlton era, and bears up well in comparison to later outfits that did qualify for major competitions. Seventeen years on, the 12 who played are dotted around the usual professions: Seamus McDonagh, publican and part-time coach; Dave O'Leary, Leeds United assistant manager; Kevin Moran, businessman and players' agent; Chris Hughton, Tottenham Hotspur assistant-manager; Ronnie Whelan, publican and ex-manager of Southend; Mark Lawrenson, media pundit; Liam Brady, director of youth development at Arsenal; Frank Stapleton, scout and media pundit; Michael Robinson, commentator on Spanish TV; Don Givens, youth coach at Arsenal; Mick Martin, sports shop proprietor and media pundit; and Davy Langan, town hall porter.

Langan doesn't begrudge any of them what they've achieved, he just wishes fate had dealt him a kinder hand. Even his career in an Ireland jersey ended ignominiously, falling off the edge of the squad shortly before history beckoned. Having started in three of the qualifiers for Euro '88, and figured in the squad for every game for which he was fit, Langan wasn't picked to travel. The omission in itself didn't hurt the player – many in the game felt it was a foregone conclusion – as much as the fact that he didn't receive any word from Jack Charlton about it.

In his autobiography, Charlton unequivocally defends his position: 'And then there was Davy Langan. He had first played for Ireland under John Giles and was coming close to the end of his career when I took over the team. In his time, he had been an excellent full-back and a good crosser of the ball. But injury problems had robbed him of his pace, and by now Chris Morris had settled into the team at right-back. Whereas Langan struggled for pace, Chris had plenty. He was brilliant in getting to the dead ball line, though once there, he was frequently awful. I mean, he couldn't cross the ball for nuts – but in every other respect, he was an exceptionally gifted full-back...

'I hadn't seen Davy for months when I bumped into him at a reception after one of our last warm-up games against Poland. I reckon he had a few drinks on board and he started giving me a bit of stick about leaving him out of the squad. More than that, he was going on at me about not phoning to tell him he was out of the squad. When a player had an injury problem and he fitted into my plans, I never hesitated to make contact. But I never felt the need to call players and tell them they were out. What was the point?'

Langan disagrees with Charlton's assessment. 'I read in his book all right that he thought my pace had gone. He never said that to my face. John Aldridge invited me up to his testimonial match at Tranmere a couple of years back and I saw Jack. He came across and was chatting to me. He shook hands and said: "I hope everything turns out all right for you." That was it.' Johnny Giles used to say to us that playing football is like being at school. As soon as you finish school, you go and you're replaced by a new class. In football it's the same, once you're dispensable, you're on your way and nobody is interested anymore.'

For Langan, the end came quickly. His knee started to give out on a more regular basis and Oxford's team started to fall apart. He moved on to Bournemouth first and then to Peterborough, the journey down the lower leagues not easing the physical strain the way that he hoped it would. A gentle jog one day at Peterborough was enough to persuade his body to call time. The surgeon took one look at his back, recommended another spinal fusion and advised him to give it up before he became a cripple. He'd heard the words before but this time he had no choice but to heed them.

Of course like so many before him, the bug didn't leave his body that easily and Langan tried to come back, playing amateur football with Merrlies Blackstone in the UCL league. In hindsight, it was a big mistake. 'It was terrible, playing on dreadful pitches, and coming up against people who because of who you are will always try to kick you. Then you get guys trying to take the mickey out of you all the time, saying: "You're finished, you're only a cripple." It's a terrible way to end up playing the game you love and it wasn't worth it.'

The rise and fall of Davy Langan was bound to give birth to a conspiracy theory or two, and the rumour went around that gambling was his downfall. At Oxford United, the players used to fraternize with jockeys from the nearby Queen's Stables, and so the story grew that Langan blew his money at the racetrack. It is a charge that he strenuously denies.

'The most I ever put on a horse was a tenner and that was on a tip from one of the lads from the Major Hern stable. Any other time, I'd put on a one pound ten pence robin. Gambling was never my problem, that's rubbish, I hate lies like that but I'm used to them now. Somebody rang up my mother a couple of months ago, and said: "Is it true Davy has a post office in Balbriggan?" Then another person came on and said: "I believe Davy has a pub out in Palmerstown." It's ridiculous the things that people will say about you.'

The truth is that his divorce from his first marriage absorbed more money that anything. 'I got divorced as well and that took a lot of my money away. The courts over here absolutely hammered me and I was paying an awful lot of maintenance money and I found it hard to save. People forget too that I wasn't on that much money in the first place. The wages then weren't what they are now.

'I was transferred for £350,000 once but in those days, the money went mostly to the clubs, we hardly saw any money out of the transfer fees. I know people at home used to think: "Jeez, 350,000, jeez, he's well off now." But I hardly got any money out of it. They spread it over three years, and the money was rubbish. I got about £1,500 a year out of the transfer and that was before the tax was taken out.

'We didn't have agents back then, we just did it on our own. Looking back, we would have been better off with agents, they'd have got more for us because they'd have known what to ask for. I was just a simple Dublin lad, I hadn't a clue about transfers and signing-on fees. With all the excitement of just being there, any transfer I went through, the first thing they said to me, I'd always just say: "Yeah, I'll have that." I never used to argue or ask for more.'

Langan's innocence and naïveté are not unique. In the era before the Professional Footballers' Association insisted on a clause stipulating that a player is entitled to a signing-on fee of 10 per cent of the overall transfer fee, it was common for clubs to try to exploit the player's lack of acumen by giving as little as he would accept. Paul McGrath, perhaps the most gifted Irish footballer ever, went to England a full decade after Langan and was equally gullible in negotiations. He signed the first paltry contract that Manchester United put in front of him, and it was only late in his career that he finally began to punch his weight when asking for wages.

McGrath overcame enormous physical handicaps to play on into his late 30s but Langan's body wasn't for stretching and reality intruded upon his existence very quickly. For the former footballer, the job options are always dreadfully limited, and Langan had spent the summers when he could have been picking up coaching badges recuperating from injuries.

'It was a shock to the system when it was all over. The day that I finished at Peterborough, I came home and said to Debbie: "What am I going to do now? I've had all these operations, nobody's going to give me a job." I just didn't know what I was going to do, and I ended up spending 18 months on the dole. I finally managed to get a job as a car-park attendant which, like the job I have now, was restricted to disabled people. I worked for a security firm after that going around in the vans, but they got rid of me once they found out about my back. With that kind of work, you might get involved in a scuffle in an emergency and they couldn't take a chance on me. "Inability to continue" was the official term they used to describe it.'

The want of a decent job is exacerbated by the lack of contact with his footballing peers. The professional footballer's is the most transient of all professions, and friendships are often the first casualties of all the moving on. 'Football is a strange job. You don't really make friends, just acquaintances, and you part ways after a while. The Irish player who I was closest to was Frank Stapleton, I was best man at his wedding but I haven't heard from Frank for a long long time now. I don't know whether he hasn't got my number or whether he's just too busy. I have found it very hard to take that I never hear from anyone. All the people who used to ring me up, I never heard from them again. Ashley Grimes called me all right but all of a sudden, it was like I didn't exist.'

A couple of years ago, sports journalist Cathal Dervan ran a campaign to try to get the FAI to organise a benefit game for Langan. They got as far as a spot on *The Joe Duffy Radio Show*, where Langan spoke about his plight. The response from the public was phenomenal, and the ex-players' fund made him a donation that eased the pressure of a few bills but there was to be no testimonial. For Langan's last knee operation, the tenth major surgery of his life, the PFA picked up the tab and spared him a couple of years on an NHS waiting list. He worries that they may not be as amenable when the knee needs another clear-out.

'I think the FAI should organise a match of some sort and split the thing between three or four of us who aren't doing so well. A few bob would help me a great deal because I'm up to me eyes in debt really. I haven't got much money coming in here – the job that I have is rubbish so the wages are rubbish. I get an extra 80 quid a month off the welfare for being disabled but I bought this house when I signed for Peterborough and I've a mortgage that's got to be paid every month.

'I look at some of the players now and I'd be reading that such and such is on 6- or 7,000 a week, and I'd think to myself that I was as good if not better than them. Imagine, I could have been earning that kind of money. That's the way things work out though, I was just born too early, and in this game, if you don't make your money while you can, you're in trouble. It's funny, you know, this was my dream. I had stars in my eyes, about making it in England and playing for my country. I never imagined throughout all those years that I could end up like this. This is a hell of a way to end up.'

Some day soon, when he thinks he's old enough to understand, the father will tell his son that when he was a lad, he was good enough to be taken on trial by

Manchester United. If that doesn't impress him, he'll point out that he was once detailed to man-mark the world's greatest player. He won't be able to show him why – the pain in his left knee precludes that – but he hopes that his son will take him at his word. Long after the cheering has stopped, the sad ballad of Davy Langan goes on.

Chapter Six

This supporting life

Part I – A grand old team

The dog comes to the door first, a mongrel stray who landed in her garden early in January six years ago. She named him Tully, after Charlie, the old Glasgow Celtic star whose unique style earned him the soubriqet 'The clown prince of footballers'. He was her favourite player ever. Maire Rua Gallagher is closing in on 70 now but she shoos the dog out of the way, and welcomes visitors with the élan of a woman who, only three weeks earlier, marched 50 blocks of Manhattan in the New York Saint Patrick's Day parade. The only legacy of her exertions is the garish green nail varnish that still adorns her fingers, and the colour neatly matches that of her sweater which bears the legend 'Celtic's number one fan.'

An unprovable boast perhaps but she has the stories to make a decent case. Maire Rua has shaken hands with Eusebio, assailed Jock Stein about the temporary absence of the Parkhead tricolour, accompanied the pre-pubescent Paddy Crerand on his first trips to Paradise, subsequently attacked the club management for allowing him to leave and been on first name terms with five generations of Celtic players. She witnessed the club's nine league titles in a row first hand, was in the airport the night Billy McNeill brought back the European Cup and from her home in Donegal, she has suffered through every failure of the last painful decade.

The kitchen of her house bears eloquent testimony to her devotion. Every free space is speckled with the twin passions of her life. A ten-year-old calendar of the last great Celtic team jostles for wall space with a poster of her beloved Daniel O'Donnell, and a collection of Celtic mugs and figurines compete for prominence on a shelf with some more O'Donnell paraphernalia. Where there aren't green and white hoops, there seems to be the smirking face of her favourite singer. If O'Donnell has been a recent infatuation, Celtic has been her life's work.

At the age of 15, Maire Rua's brother Manus brought her to Scotland for the potato-picking season, down the well-worn path of the Donegal migrant worker. They left their mother's house in Bunbeg at five in the morning to catch a bus from the old schoolhouse which would take them as far as Derry, and the train. The old schoolhouse is boarded up now and the bus no longer runs. From the window of her kitchen, Maire can see the daily commuter flight from Glasgow touch down at the tiny airstrip that lips the strand at the other side of the bay. Her few visits a year to Parkhead are made by air now too.

'Back then we had to go to try and make some money because there was no jobs here. It was hard leaving your nice house to go into these places but there was nothing else for us. The first time I went I was scared, surely. The farthest I'd ever travelled before was the 12 miles to Dunloe for to get my passport photo taken. There was a group of seven or eight of us travelled from this townland here and everything seemed so huge over there.

'My brother had been over the year before and he gave me an idea of what was in front of me. That was the way it went back then, the older ones took the younger ones over because they knew what it was like. They gave us an idea of what was in front of us. We had to lie on straw at night in these big botties with just a couple of blankets to keep warm. It was really rough but when you're young you're able for that kind of hardship.

'We were all Irish together in it. We used to keep warm by

singing songs around the fire at night. It was tough but we used to have good craic. The season started off on 4 June up in Ayrshire because that's where the potatoes would be ripe first and it finished up in Perthshire around November. When the season was over you could come home or else stay to do other jobs like dressing the potatoes but only if you were strong enough to put up with the cold of the winter.'

Eavesdropping adult conversations about football had caused the teenage Maire to think her elders were persistently discussing some exotic entity called 'Celtic-Rangers'. Only after a time in Scotland did she decipher the proper meaning of what they were saying, and the talk of Celtic was so incessant among the emigrants that she couldn't help but become smitten herself. At the beginning of her exile, she used to blow all her disposable income on trips to the pictures but she soon found a better outlet for her Saturday afternoons.

'There was a man from Belfast in the name of Charlie Tully came to Celtic, and once I heard he was Irish, I really started getting involved. The first game I went to was a New Year's Day match against Rangers, and Celtic got beat 4–0. I knew nothing about the game, all I could see was people. There were 132,000 at the match and I had never seen so many people in my life before. I asked the man beside me which one was Charlie Tully, and I had eyes for nobody but Charlie after that.'

Her second game was the 1951 Scottish Cup final. Celtic beat Motherwell 1-0 that day and afterwards, Maire Rua and her friends from work stood sentry outside Ferrari's restaurant in Buchanan Street where the victorious team would traditionally come for their post-match meal. Her memory of the day is vivid enough for her to recall that Cotter's was the name of the bus which ferried the players through the waiting throng.

'The gaffer that we had knew somebody involved in Celtic because he used to go to all the matches, and he knew that the players used to dine in Ferrari's. We took the mini-bus that we had up there but nobody was getting in. Then, whatever way the pushing went, I landed inside the door and the first man I seen was Jimmy Mallon. I said to him: "I would like to meet Charlie Tully," and he went away and brought him back.

'That was the first time I ever met Charlie and he said to me: "Are you the girl who's been writing me all the letters off the farm?" I says "I am, and I'm so glad to meet you." Soon I got to meet all the team, and after that I was Celtic-daft. I travelled all over Scotland to see them play and I knew all the players for years to come. Once I was bit by Celtic, there was no place like Scotland for me.'

After a few years on the potato-picking circuit, Maire Rua got a job as a bus conductor in a Glasgow garage where the workers divided neatly along Celtic and Rangers lines. Her best friend on the buses was a Protestant Rangers fan called Gracie Ferguson. 'She would support any team who would beat Celtic and I would support any team who would beat Rangers but we were still the best of pals. You see, the Rangers fans are not all bad. There's bad and good in them if you take them the right way.' To this day, Maire and Gracie spend a week every summer holidaying together in the Scottish Highlands.

Maire's time on the buses coincided with the last throes of an era when professional footballers still got the bus to work. Very often, her passengers would be the people she idolised or despised every weekend. But whether the player carrying the gear bag was a Celt or a Ger, she would never take their fares. In her eyes, they were all stars. This ecumenical view of the Rangers players didn't always extend to their supporters. If Gracie Ferguson showed Maire the humane face of their fans, others were not so kind.

'One day, I was walking down from the match with this boy from Burtonport, and we walked along a road we shouldn't have. That day, the game had finished 4-4 but it was Rangers day because they had come back to draw in the last ten minutes. When I came through the end of this Rangers' crowd, a bottle was thrown and it hit me on the head. But I was very proud of what I done, I turned around and said: "You're only a crowd of animals hitting a woman on the head." I walked out of there with my knees trembling and blood on my head.

'It was always worse up at Ibrox though, it was never very homely up there. We were always afraid coming out of their place because it wasn't like at Parkhead where the Rangers would go one way and we'd go the other. At Ibrox sometimes the two would meet along Coupland Road, and you'd always be afraid of getting a wee doing especially me who had my mouth open all the time.

'Coming down from Parkhead could be bad too. Two Rangers women caught each end of my scarf one day and spun me round 'til I fell but that was nothing next to the time I got cut with a blade, and had my purse robbed off me by more Rangers fans. I got a fair few doings all right, including a belt of a fish supper in the face off a woman. I always say it was my own fault. I talked back to them you see, I would never give in.'

Altercations like that exaggerated Maire Rua's reputation and gave birth to apocryphal tales about her activities. A story did the rounds that when her bus would pull up at Paisley Cross, she would stand at the door and shout, 'Celtic supporters only please'. 'Of course, that wasn't true, I would have got my books off the buses if it was.'

For the Irish in exile, Celtic was a focal point, the tricolour over Parkhead an important little piece of home. The entire environment was geared towards interacting with fellow emigrants, and in the Celtic supporters' clubs, the songs they sang were songs of Ireland, 'Kevin Barry', 'James Connolly' and 'Home to Donegal'. Taking her place on the terrace known as 'The Jungle' every second Saturday, Maire could count on meeting the same faces and hearing the familiar Donegal accents. The football was really only the half of it.

'It was a meeting place for us and the tricolour in particular was always a great comfort. I remember one time when it was down for a couple of months, I went up to Jock Stein and said: "What's wrong with the tricolour?" He said: "What do you mean?" And I said: "The tricolour hasn't been flying above Parkhead for nearly two months." When he told me that it was away getting repairs, I said: "Jock Stein, just tell me the truth, sure you have thousands of them flags." Anyway, I came back the following Saturday and the tricolour was there again.'

Through the years, Maire struck up a friendship with another Donegal native, Sara Tim Crerand and watched her boy Paddy grow up to wear the jersey himself. Even when he left for Manchester United, they'd often get the train south to support him at Old Trafford.

'When he was a wee boy, Paddy used to go up to Parkhead and I was a big star to him because I knew Tully and all them, and I'd bring Paddy over to meet them. With him being a wee lad and all, he thought this was great. Then of course, he became a great player himself and I was very angry when Paddy left Celtic. I thought he should never have left but it was just things went wrong.

'We never knew the ins and outs of it. Somebody told me once that it was Sean Fallon's fault and I don't know whether it was or not but I went up to Parkhead to see. When Sean Fallon came out, I grabbed him and said: "It's your fault that Paddy Crerand's away from Celtic today, and if you go down to the Gorbals, the boys will sort you out." I was sorry about that after because I found out later that it wasn't Sean's fault at all. Sean was a great Celtic man himself but we had to blame somebody.'

The May night in 1968 when Paddy Crerand won his European Cup medal with Manchester United, Maire and Sara Tim were in the stands at Wembley. Afterwards, they waited outside to greet him not knowing that he was suffering badly from dehydration. 'I made for Paddy because I knew him since he was a child but he was as white as a sheet. Bobby Charlton told me: "Leave Paddy alone, he's sick." I told Charlton to shut up. I knew Paddy long before him and I wanted to give him a hug. I didn't know that he really was sick and had to go to the hospital but I never liked that Bobby Charlton anyway.'

Maire's 33 years in Scotland dovetailed with some of Celtic's purplest patches. Over time, she progressed from her place in 'The Jungle' to a season ticket in the stands, alongside Sara Tim. From those vantage points, she revelled in their nine leagues in a row – that caused Jock Stein to joke that his team would have to enter the English league to encounter some real competition – and her biggest regret is giving up a seat on a plane bound for the European Cup final in Lisbon in 1967.

'Even though he was a Rangers fan, my boss gave me a few days off to go, and I booked my ticket with Sara Tim. I don't know what came over me but I was afraid to go. I've been to America six times but I've never been to Europe, and I was too scared to go. The game was on a Thursday evening, and it was a holy day of obligation. I went up to Mass and afterwards I met this boy and we went off to watch the match together. When it was over, I still couldn't believe that Celtic had won. I thought it must be a dream.'

The morning after the game, Maire posted a colour newspaper photograph of the victorious Celtic team on the front window of her bus as she did her rounds. Nobody asked her to take it down.

Back in Donegal for 17 years now, her trips across have dwindled from once a month in the beginning to three or four a year, and the last team she could claim genuine kinship with was that of Packie Bonner, Paul McStay and Peter Grant. 'Them were boys who were playing for the jumper just like Tully and that crowd before them, their hearts were in Celtic. With the team these days, there's too much coming and going. I can't keep up with all the changes, a fella is there one day and gone the next, there's no point in having a favourite because you don't know when they'll be gone. I blame the tops who are running the club. They're not the same as James McGroary and Kelly used to be. It's too much of a business now, it seems to be all about money.'

When she travels to Parkhead these days, she is even more saddened by the distance between the players and the fans, as the interaction between the two that she and her peers once enjoyed has disappeared forever.

'The last time I was over there we were waiting for the players to come out to us but we saw none. It's all changed so much. Before, the players would come out and they'd all talk to us and sign autographs. It was all very friendly but it's all so different now. They don't mix with the fans like they used to. Back then, they used to even come into the same pubs as us like Michael Heraghty's in the Gorbals.'

As Celtic's star fell in recent years, Daniel O'Donnell's rose inexorably and for Maire at least, that was some compensation. But when O'Donnell played at the Point Depot in Dublin on 11 April 1998, Maire Rua was absent for the first time that anyone can remember. Needs must. Attending the concert would have meant not being home in time to watch the Old Firm derby in her neighbour Charlie Doherty's house the following afternoon. She loves them both equally but on this day, Celtic's need was more pressing, and the tug of the jersey was greater. 'I have to see this game because this will be our turn to sing "You'll never make it ten".'

Celtic lost the match that April afternoon but won the war. Maire Rua didn't have to wait long for her wish to be granted.

Part II – For my father's country

It's the build-up to a friendly international between Wales and Ireland and the location is a Cardiff public house called The Philharmonic . The date is 11 February 1997. The scene is a men's toilet where two Irish fans are standing at the urinals. One of them has an English accent and is wearing an Ireland jersey. The other is from Dublin.

'All right, mate?' says the English-born supporter.

The Dubliner is perturbed by this. He stares hard at his questioner, taking in the green jersey, the accent, and suddenly he asks:

'Are youse for or against us?'

'What the hell's that supposed to mean?' replies the Londoner, whose passport stamps stand witness to the distances he has travelled in support of the Irish soccer team.

The debate ends there. The Dubliner sets upon his fellow supporter, punching and kicking him until he has two black eyes, severe bruising and an injured neck; his punishment for the crime of being an Ireland fan with an English accent.

In the wider world of football where violence is not a rarity, it was an unremarkable incident, but for every second and third generation Irish fan, it was a worst nightmare finally coming true.

For this subsection of the Irish support, every Ireland game is an away fixture yet, travelling the globe in support of the country of their mothers and fathers, they still have to suffer ignorant taunts. Their accents give away their origins quickly enough, and a minority of Irish fans have often seemed eager to capitalise on their difference. If the verbal lashings were annoying but tolerable, they always feared that some day the talking would give way to a physical assault. Cardiff was an incident waiting to happen.

Pat Redmond was the victim of the savage and cowardly attack that evening. The son of a Kildare man who emigrated to London in 1947 to work as a nurse, Redmond's credentials are impeccable. 'Are youse for or against us?' Never mind Giants Stadium in '94 or Stuttgart in '88 or Italia '90, Redmond had been one of the tiny band of Irish fans, first or second generation, to travel to Israel in 1983 to see Eoin Hand's team lose 3-0 in another friendly, at a time when it was neither fashionable nor cheap to do so. When the National Front attacked the Black Lion pub in Kilburn before Ireland's 1-1 draw with England at Wembley in 1991, Redmond had to receive stitches after being hit by a flying brick. 'Are youse for or against us?' indeed.

The idea for a London branch of the Republic of Ireland Soccer Supporters' Club was conceived in 1983. Up until then, Irish fans would casually bump into each other at Heathrow and Gatwick airports as they caught flights to the same European destinations in pursuit of their team. After one such trip to Iceland, it was decided by Pat Redmond, amongst others, that it would be a good idea to organise themselves onto a more formal footing. Gerry Lappin, a Longford native, was the first chairman, and writing in the Irish edition of *The Sunday Times*, Peter Carbery, a journalist and member of the supporters' club, best summed up the origins of the new grouping.

'A few dozen fans turned up at the first meeting,' wrote Carbery. 'As the song goes, there were men from Dublin and from Cork – but most were young, second generation Irish like Pat Redmond, part of the generation born to those who had left Ireland in the '50s and early '60s. They were more confident of their identity and ready to express it in their support for their team. A decade earlier, it would have been a brave or foolhardy action to have "come out" in a Britain still reeling from the Guildford and Birmingham pub bombings, and openly hostile to any celebration of Irishness. Times had changed however.'

In reality, these people could not really have supported any other team. Their families may have been physically domiciled in England but Ireland remained the spiritual home. Trips back to see their relatives took on the status of annual pilgrimages, and for the rest of the year, the houses they lived in teemed with Irishness. When visitors came around, they, and the songs and stories they brought with them, were invariably Irish too.

Fathers would spend Sunday afternoons with their ears up to the wireless, harkening a barely audible Radio Eireann signal, trying to listen to a Gaelic football or hurling commentary. *The Irish Post* was the staple read every week along with, when the shops had it, the old *Sunday Press* from Dublin. Although these people lived in England, the bonds of the Irish community were so adhesive that Maurice McCrohan, the 34 year-old-son of a Cork mother and Kerry father, can honestly say that when he left his North London school at 18, he was shocked at just how cosmopolitan the rest of London was.

Tony Booth, club chairman for the last 11 years, missed that first meeting but at the second, in the function room of the Prince of Wales' Feathers in Warren Street, he was voted on to the committee. His family circumstances are almost identical to Pat Redmond's. His mother, Gwen Blennerhasset, came across from Kerry in the post-war years to train to be a nurse. She married an Englishman but instilled in her son a peculiar sense of Irish nationalism.

'I remember in 1966 the World Cup finals were on in

England, and for a lot of people in my generation, that is their first memory of football. I was 13 years old and no different. I had taken no great interest in football until then but I watched the final with my mother and she was desperately supporting West Germany. I asked her why, and she said simply: "Because they're playing England." It follows on from there that in France this summer, I will have 31 other teams to support rather than England.

'But back then when I walked into the second supporters club meeting, I felt I had to show my credentials. I felt like I nearly had to produce a long birth certificate because for those who speak with an English accent, you almost have to create your own identity for other people's benefit. You have to wear the colours, you have to show the ticket stub from such and such a game, say the name of some village in Galway that you wouldn't know unless you had really heard of it. But we have pink, brown and black people in our club who are all Irish. We are totally multi-ethnic, multi-religious but all Irish. It's a great melting pot that we have.'

The basic premise for the new organisation was sound. Collectively, they could bargain with airlines, hotels and travel agents to get better deals when travelling abroad, and for match tickets, it made more sense for one voice to be talking to the FAI on behalf of a couple of hundred. Monthly meetings were established, at which tickets could be distributed, details of trips announced and match videos shown. The club even negotiated a deal direct with kit manufacturers so that members could buy replica jerseys at a reduced rate. Seamus McDonagh was the first honorary president, to be succeeded by Chris Hughton, and most recently, Kenny Cunningham.

The timing for the new organisation was particularly good. The foundation preceded the success of the Charlton era, and London in the '80s was such a boom town that the members would have had more disposable income than most to spend on traversing Europe behind their team. 'The branch was definitely founded at the right time,' says Tony Booth. 'We'd been unlucky not to qualify on a couple of occasions in the early '80s but the games weren't anywhere near sell-outs so we could still get tickets. If the club had been formed during the high point of the Jack Charlton era, we would only have been able to get three tickets for every home game, and wouldn't have had the opportunity to support the team in such numbers.'

At its peak in the early '90s, the London branch had over 800 members, double the number of its Dublin counterpart at the same time. The numbers have levelled off now to somewhere above 600 but the commitment hasn't waned. Booth is one of several London-Irish supporters who travelled to Perth in Scotland to see the Under-16 team win the European Championships in May 1998. The same month, he came to Dublin twice in six days to see Paul McGrath's testimonial, and Ireland's friendly against Mexico. He is a good example of the type of die-hards who join the club but he is only one of many. Even on that dreadful night in Cardiff, 20 per cent of the Irish support had driven down the M3 from London.

'I've been lucky because of the accent,' says Booth. 'It allowed me to go to the games in Northern Ireland because I ran less of a risk of getting recognised as a Republic of Ireland supporter than say somebody from Dublin would have. I remember particularly the game when Alan McLoughlin scored at Windsor Park in 1993. Because of security restrictions, there were no tickets available for Republic fans but we managed to get a couple. I was sitting next to my mate Sean and neither of us were wearing any colours. When the goal went in, the goal that would take us to America, we just sat on our hands, didn't even smile.'

The accent has its uses then, but they are surely outweighed by the hassle that it brings. Although there were very few negative vibes towards the London-Irish brigade in the early years, those within the club feel that something changed around 1988 when Ray Houghton's goal against England catapulted the Irish team into a different universe, and quadrupled the numbers who were travelling to away matches in particular.

'It was fine in the early days because there tended to be a lot more second generation than soccer fans from Dublin.'

says Maurice McCrohan. 'It all started to change with the popularity of 1988 and we started to get a lot more: "What are youse doing here? Are England not playing this weekend?" I suppose that we were puzzled at first although we had suspected that it might come some day.

'It was funny because the majority of the team in that era were from the same type of background as me. They had much more in common with the second generation than they would have had with somebody who grew up in Dublin. We always tried to avoid the arguments because we felt here's a pub full of Irish fans, if it gets a bit heated, I don't think the rest of the pub are going to back up the people with the English accents. So we tried to deflate it with a bit of banter and avoided arguments by using our wits.'

McCrohan touches on the greatest irony of all this. If any of the London-Irish fans had been talented enough footballers, they would of course have been playing for, and not just supporting, Ireland. In which case, the very same people who were ridiculing their accents and their ancestry would have revered them, regardless of their birthplace.

'Not everyone held out a welcome for the diaspora,' wrote Peter Carbery. 'Mary Robinson may have talked of placing candles in windows back at the Phoenix Park, but in bars and hotels across Europe, conversations between Irish-based fans and those born and raised in England would invariably turn to one subject. "Wha' are youse doin' over here? Why aren't youse following England? Sure, youse aren't Irish at all." '

The questions came hand in glove with insults which were varied and hurtful. 'Plastic Paddy' was probably the most common term of abuse but others weren't averse to calling members of the London branch, 'Brits' and 'Tans'. Each is bad in its own way but 'Tans', short for 'Black and Tans', an auxiliary British paramilitary force with a reputation for lawless behaviour and merciless killing, sent into Ireland with a licence to wreak havoc in 1920, was particularly offensive.

More irony. Maurice McCrohan went to Finchley Catholic High School in North London, an establishment so rabidly

Irish that when the British Army came on a recruitment drive during the IRA hunger strikes in 1981, some pupils cut balaclavas out of plastic bags, placed them over their heads, and made sniper gestures. They also goaded the young British soldiers that their Irish cousins were going to get them.

They dealt with the insults in different ways. In Turkey one time, they initiated a song contest. Who knew more songs? The Irish or the London-Irish? The Irish usually fell silent by the third verse, and there could really only be one winner. By the end of the night, the chant went up: 'London-Irish know the words.'

There were other ways of establishing supremacy too. Some opted to discuss family trees and the blight of emigration to shame their detractors while others resorted to question and answer sessions about the Irish team BC (Before Charlton) – a very successful method of exposing the bandwagon jumpers. In Hungary one evening, they even adopted a response of their own. Borrowing heavily from the old Millwall standard, they sang: 'We are Irish, London-Irish, no one likes us, we don't care.' In the same vein, one set of fans used to carry a tricolour daubed with the slogan: 'Ilford Plastic Paddies on Tour'.

'There was lots of things we would do,' says Maurice McCrohan. 'We used to say: "Most of you lot go around the place dressed in Manchester United and Liverpool jerseys all the time. Even if we were English, then can you explain why you go over supporting English football every week?" I'm a bit mellower now because I'm living here in Dublin but my friends back in London constantly discuss the contradictions involved. The perception over there is that it is more Dubliners having a go than people from any other county. I think somebody in our number dubbed the Dubliners "the master race" because they seem to think they're purer Irish than anybody else.'

Tony Booth is less inclined to lay the blame at the door of any one set of supporters but he shares the anger. 'It does hurt me because I can't help the way that I speak. I've been to places to support Ireland where somebody who is going to have a go at me about my accent has never been to. I've spent my hard-earned money trying to support Ireland, and that gets at me. I suppose I can understand it a bit because if you are a born and bred Dub, your perception of a person with an English accent might be negative because of history.

'But as soon as I open my mouth, I say: "I was in such and such a place, did you go to that game?" And the reply will almost always be: "Nah, I don't usually go to away matches." It's almost like I have to wear the badges round my hat and sew the labels into my duffle bag or keep showing the stamps in my passport to convince people of my sincerity. I have an Irish passport so I'm an alien in England. I have an immigration stamp on my passport that was given to me the last time I flew into Heathrow. I'm treated like an alien there and yet I have to put up with people asking me why I'm supporting Ireland.'

For the Irish fan living and working in London, there is the added pressure of having to explain to English work-mates and friends why they don't support the country in which they were born. Tony Booth has often thought of keeping his foreign travels with Ireland to himself but often finds his natural inclination to talk about what a wonderful time he's had in Lithuania/Luxembourg/Latvia means he can't.

'My English work-mates' attitude to me is different than it would be if I was a true-blue Brit. They know that I'm not supporting England, and they know that I want them to lose. I'm not rude to people about it, and we generally end up having the same sort of banter you might get between a City and a United fan in Manchester. That said, I don't think it's easy being Irish in England if you are any way sensitive, and I don't think it's unreasonable to be sensitive. I don't go slagging off English people for what they are, and I don't see why me or my kind should have to tolerate it in the other direction.'

In any case, it would be difficult for Booth to keep his cover. When somebody tells an Irish joke in his presence, he bristles and always ask the jester not to repeat the offence. In the midst of the brouhaha about England's ticket allocation for France '98, he wrote a letter to *The Times* of London, reminding them that there is always a dearth of tickets at World Cups. And after the Lansdowne Riot in 1995, Booth challenged David Mellor on Radio Five Live, after the former Tory minister suggested that the crowd trouble had more to do with Irish incompetence than English hooliganism. In the wake of the Redmond incident, he made his presence felt on the Irish airwaves too.

'The incident in Cardiff was something that we wanted to highlight because we wanted to nip it in the bud,' says Booth. 'To the best of my knowledge, it was unique, a once-off. I don't know whether the geezer who did this to Pat was going to his first match or what, but we wanted to make sure it won't happen again.'

In terms of the type of people following the Republic of Ireland over the last decade, the wheel appears to have turned full circle. The failure to qualify for Euro '96 and France '98, and an extended run of poor form at senior level, while lamentable, has served to weed out the fair weather supporters. Those fans who make the trips to Skopje, Split and Belgrade as Ireland attempt to qualify for the European championships over the next two years will most likely be of the same vintage as those who supported the team pre '88. These have always been the sort to accept the London-Irish branch's bona fides quicker than most.

'Over time you get to know the faces and people get to know you from being at the games,' says Maurice McCrohan. 'They remember that they met you that time in Brussels or Budapest or wherever and they know that you are a genuine fan, and even if they did resent you before, they realise that you are just as committed as them.'

And when ignorance does rear its ugly head again in the coming years, the London-Irish fans will resort to the old standard: 'An Irish fan with an English accent?' says Tony Booth. 'Well, being born in a stable wouldn't make me a horse now, would it?'

Chapter Seven

Cross channel chat

It was one of the most poignant Irish sports stories of the decade. With his 22-man squad billeted in Malta in preparation for the 1990 World Cup, Jack Charlton decided to make a last minute change of personnel. Alan McLoughlin, the bright young Swindon mid-fielder, was called up to replace Gary Waddock who was older and more experienced but not considered to be as much of an attacking force. At that time, the Irish team were beginning to impact on the wider world and the story was big news in Britain too. After all, Ireland were preparing to play England in their first group game, so any potentially negative vibes emanating from the Irish camp were worth reporting.

On his return to London, Gary Waddock was besieged by offers from English tabloids. He refused them all and the only phone call he took was from Bob Hennessy, an Irish journalist long domiciled in England whom Waddock had known since he first broke through to the youths team. 'I had three phone numbers for him, I eventually ferreted him out, and he spoke. Jack sent him home on the plane and he was in tears. Two days later, he gave me the interview and the guy never once had a go, he was just hurt and choked by it all. I know that he was offered huge money by a London paper to dish the dirt but he wouldn't do that. For nothing, he gave me the quotes about how hurt he was and I wrote it in the *Evening Herald*.'

Bob Hennessy is too modest to say so himself but Gary Waddock spoke to him in preference to all others because he trusted him. Hennessy is on first name terms with more Irish professional footballers than any other journalist in these islands. He has compiled columns on the subject of the Irish in Britain for over 30 years, and his work has appeared in every major Irish newspaper. Still, he is probably more famous in Iceland where his twice weekly contributions to *Morgunbladdid*, that country's most popular morning paper, have acquired a cult status. If he is Iceland's eyes and ears in the English game, his contribution towards the cause of the Irish in Britain is more prosaic. He might be described as a living, breathing archive of Irish soccer's recent history except that it would play down the fact that he is a work in progress, constantly upgrading the 350 and more files he has on individual players.

Robbie Keane's emergence in the Wolves' first team on the first day of the 1997/98 season caught almost every Irish soccer writer unawares, as the 17-year-old Dubliner had never even made the bench before. But Bob Hennessy had talked to Keane on the phone four days before his senior début for a piece for the English edition of the *Sunday Independent*. He'd got the boy's name and number from another Irish youngster at Wolves and acted accordingly. When he rang the digs, Keane answered the phone himself and talked freely. While Keane was scoring two goals against Norwich City that Saturday afternoon, the paper was already printing the first ever interview with him. A week later, the Wolves management put a temporary gag on Keane talking to the press but even during that time, he never refused a phone call from Hennessy.

The phone is Hennessy's forte. It is his medium. This interview could have been done in person on several different occasions but instead was conducted over the phone. It seemed only right because the phone is where Bob Hennessy spends his days, coaxing numbers from people, dragging words from tongue-tied young footballers and constantly sniffing out different angles which he can flog to the Irish papers. Indeed he is such a consummate performer on the phone that he actually seems less than loquacious when you meet him in person.

His proficiency with phone in hand means that he has the best contacts book in the game and the same can be said of the files he keeps. His system is amazingly comprehensive. After Paul McGrath announced his formal retirement from the game in April 1998, Hennessy opened the file he had on the player. A tiny paragraph from the *Evening Press* detailing the player's initial sale to Manchester United 16 years before was pasted on to the outside of one of the two bulging folders marked 'McGrath'. Inside, there were cuttings from seemingly every newspaper and periodical imaginable right up to March of that year. Double page spreads from Irish tabloids nestled next to Q and A's from *Shoot*, and all the glowing hymns of praise were housed in the same place as the various tabloid exposés about his private life. In amongst it all was a Xerox copy of McGrath's first boot contract with Adidas which somebody faxed Hennessy as a tip-off.

The McGrath collection epitomises the comprehensive and painstaking approach he has to research. Moreover, he applies the same attention to detail with Third Division and even non-league players as he does to established internationals. He has a working relationship with a correspondent in just about every regional paper in Britain so he will regularly be faxed copies of articles about Irish players from publications in the four corners of the country. No other Irish journalist can claim to have a cuttings archive like this, and should the FAI ever get around to constructing a Hall of Fame type museum, Hennessy's loft could form the backbone of it.

In this age of circulation wars and marketing devices, it has become the stuff of tabloid hyperbole for certain journalists to appropriate titles to themselves such as 'the voice of Irish soccer'. Bob Hennessy would never, ever allow himself to be described in that way. He has no ego – often admitting he cannot write the huge full page interviews which dominate contemporary sports coverage – but this is the moniker which fits him best. Others may make lofty claims on their own behalf; Bob Hennessy life's work speaks for itself.

Bob Hennessy grew up on Donore Avenue in Dublin's south inner city. Having attended St Catherine's Primary school, he passed a voice test to become a chorister in St Patrick's Cathedral which entitled him to reduced fees for attending the secondary school attached to the church. To this day, the only passion in his life to compare with soccer is his continuing involvement with a male voice choir. At St Patrick's, singing went hand in glove with education, and every Sunday morning, Hennessy and his compeers sang at service in Trinity College.

St Patrick's was a hockey academy too and though he dabbled in the game, it never took hold of him like soccer did. Having started out playing for the Boys' Brigade, he joined the YMCA and eventually a group of lads he met there stayed together to enter a team in the United Churches' League. A lightly-built but quick inside forward, Hennessy did well enough at that level to gain representative honours for the UCL. 'I played against Northern Ireland at Dalymount Park when I was about 16. The game was played under lights and I thought the whole event was just fantastic, the best thing ever.'

Back then scouting was not the scientific process it is now and there was a haphazard air to any opportunities that befell young players. 'I always wanted to be a footballer, and I never really know how it happened but somebody suggested that I contact Southend United. I don't know why, I don't know what it was, whether it was somebody standing on the line or what, but anyway I wrote off, and I went over on trial. This would have been around 1962 or '63, and I combined the trip to Southend with a holiday in London.'

His three weeks at Roots Hall quickly robbed him of any notions about the professional game. 'At the end of it all, a guy called Ernie Shepherd told me to go back to Dublin and they'd keep track on me. I hadn't been confident enough. I stood in awe of the other English boys putting out the towels in the morning, and running errands. I was too quiet, and in training, it was the first time that somebody said to me: "Don't chase the ball, watch the man." Like a fool I was chasing after the ball so they stopped me doing that. I always remember that incident. Ironically my wife Lynda had grown up going to Southend games with her father. Anyway, I enjoyed the experience, it was a nice little taster.'

Close to 40 years later, much of his business is ringing up new arrivals who might be suffering from the same trepidation as afflicted him. Most probably away from home for the first time, living in a strange city that will often appear cold and inhospitable, loneliness can often handicap even the most talented individuals. When he rings up any young Irish apprentice, Hennessy is always conscious of the fact that, more than just a journalist, he is also perhaps a warm, familiar accent which may break the monotony of a long evening in for an unhappy youngster.

By that stage of his own teenhood, Hennessy had left school for a job as a copy boy in Independent Newspapers. 'I was running errands and proofreading on the *Irish Independent*, and that really triggered a feeling for newspapers in me. There used to be a famous football man in there called Kieran Kenealy, he was the football scribe, and I used to read his copy and check it for errors. I loved the whole business. I was there the night the copy came down the chute about Liam Whelan dying in the Munich air crash. In the setting room where I worked, I opened up the page and handed it to the overseer.'

His affection for the job was soon undermined by a union official who objected to him getting an apprenticeship because his father wasn't in the trade. Effectively, he was told he had no future in the business and he ended up selling carbon paper and typewriter ribbons for a company called Royal Gold. If he left newspapers at that stage, newspapers never quite left him. He continued to devour newspapers daily while confessing that throughout his entire adult life, he hadn't managed to read five books. One year in the typewriter trade was followed by emigration to London, his brief and ill-fated dalliance with Southend

United not having diminished his fascination with the place.

Like so many before and after him, Hennessy took the boat from Dún Laoghaire, and caught a train to Euston on the other side. Checking into the YMCA on Great Russell Street, he had £12 in his pocket and a suitcase, the inside of which he had carefully festooned with photographs of Sophia Loren. Having quickly secured a clerical job, he began his life in the new world.

'I remember my mother saying to me, "You think the streets of London are paved with gold and they'll pay you £40 a week and all that." But there was a lot of Irish lads coming to London in those days, to do trades or to work in big stores, and it was a great time. This was the era of the Beatles and The Rolling Stones, all cuban heels and long hair. Across the road from the YMCA was the Guitar Club and up the road, you had the Irish club. It was marvellous. I shared a room with another Dublin lad called Percy Griffin and a cripple from Saigon who worked for the BBC as a translator.

'Everybody stayed there back then. I remember there was a budding ballet star living with us called Wayne Sleep. It was only £2.50 a week, cheap rent. And if you stayed out all night, you made sure you disturbed your bed in the morning so the maid who came in the next day didn't tell on you. We used to string football boot laces across the room to hang up our nylon drip dry shirts, and we'd have the Seekers and the Stones bellowing out the whole time. Saturday mornings, we'd go up Oxford Street to buy a bag of broken biscuits then go down to one of the coffee bars in Soho.'

Saturday afternoons were usually reserved for standing on the terraces at Loftus Road or Highbury, both of which were convenient on the Central Line. Some weekends, however, his own playing career took preference over spectating. His first English club was called London Irish, a loose amalgam of former Boys' Brigade members who played in the Kent League. He wasn't long there when he was invited to move up a grade by signing for Southall in the Athenian League.

'That was the first time I ever got money for playing. We

got a fiver a week but it was supposed to be amateur, so sometimes they'd leave the money in your boots. Other times, they'd go to extraordinary lengths to cover it up. The manager would say to a guy "I'll bet you a fiver you can't jump over that bucket there." The guy would jump over it and the manager would give him the fiver. That was how you got your payment.'

The first professional game he attended was the 1964 FA Cup final between Preston North End and West Ham United. As soon as the date is out of his mouth, a torrent of trivia flows after it; that the Irish international Alan Kelly senior was in goal for Preston, that Howard Kendall was playing and that seven of the West Ham team had surnames which began with the initial B. Hennessy's recall of events, and memory for names is phenomenal. In most conversations with him, the mention of a name will often cause an instant digression. Talking about his love for newspapers, he mentions Harry Stephenson, a family friend who worked in the *Evening Herald*, before immediately appending some information about Harry's brother Alec's career as a tricky winger with Everton in the '30s and '40s.

Through those first years in London, Hennessy followed football religiously without ever trying to write anything about it. That all changed when, on a trip home to Dublin, he went into Eason's on O'Connell Street and bought a new Irish publication called *Soccer Reporter*. 'I saw that the editor was Alan Dalton, and I thought that must be the Alan Dalton I went to school with, and true enough it was. I rang him, and said I'd do an article. The first one I wrote was on Damien Richardson, a young Dublin player down at Gillingham. I wrote that and afterwards Alan suggested I do a monthly column of snippets about the Irish in England which they called "Cross Channel Chat".'

The relationship with Dalton's magazine and Richardson have both endured. The column, now called 'Bob Hennessy's Notebook' appears in Dalton's present publication *Irish Soccer*, while Richardson, now manager of Shelbourne in the National League of Ireland, still rings Bob regularly seeking information on potential purchases in the

English game. In this, he is not alone. Most of the serious Irish clubs have been in contact at some stage, and Bob can claim involvement in such managerial appointments as Richardson and Eamon O'Keefe at Cork City and most recently, Don O'Riordan at Galway United.

While his initial contributions to *Soccer Reporter* began to yield more work for Irish publications, he continued to hold down a day job in the Automobile Association. Although soccer writing was his love, he couldn't afford to live off it. 'At night, I was ringing up people like Tony Grealish for interviews, while during the day I was involved in the Five Star Vehicle recovery programme, helping to bring members' cars back from the continent after they had broken down. Of course, I wouldn't know five things that are under the bonnet of a car but it was a laugh for a few years, sorting out towage in Germany and broken windscreens in France.'

The AA was good fun for a while but journalism remained the dream. To this end, he took a job as an editorial assistant in Press Association which involved him selling stories to local papers and radio stations all over Britain. It was a journalistic environment but it wasn't journalism. After several applications for jobs in the sports department of PA were turned down, he tried to get a job in the racing section as a typist because the money was better. Again, he had no joy.

'The racing editor collared me one day on the steps of PA, and said: "Hennessy, you're the chap who applied for a job as a typist, well we saw your application and we have a vacancy on the outside racing staff if you're interested." Racing was something where I just flicked over the page, I had no interest in it whatsoever but I told him the next day I'd take it.

'All I was doing was assisting Dai Davies, this legend in racing circles, in getting distances, pink slips and the results of enquiries. In the press room then, I was always earwigging so that the guys in *The Standard* or *The Express* didn't have something we didn't have, because there was a lot of competition. I hadn't a clue about racing but I had a good memory and I fell into it. The wage was good and there were generous days off.'

The PA working conditions allowed him plenty of time to pursue his interest in the Irish in Britain, and he continued to contribute to various publications having come up with his own unique style of approaching players. 'My policy was and still is to contact young lads who move over here and might be lonely in digs. I ring them up and have a chat. I ask them who's in their family back home and who helped them to get here. I just look to get enough information for a paragraph. I try and get that printed and then I send them a copy of the magazine or the paper it was in.

'A month or two later, I'd ring again, scribble another few lines. By then he might be in the reserves or may even have scored a few goals. Then I write about that and this would then lead hopefully to "Bob I'm in the first team" next time around. A year later it's "Bob, I've got my first professional contract or an international call-up." I always hope that they might remember that years before, you wrote two paragraphs about them when nobody knew them and act accordingly. My style is based solely on courtesy and goodwill.'

In those days, soccer didn't receive the saturation media coverage that it does now, and Hennessy was one of the few journalists writing regularly about the Irish players in Britain during an era before the FAI got a proper handle on just who the Irish abroad were. Over the last couple of years, Mick McCarthy's assistant, Ian Evans, and the under-age coach, Brian Kerr, have dedicated themselves to trawling the minor leagues of the English game in a bid to keep an eye on emerging Irish talent while hoping to unearth one or two more who nobody had known about. Hennessy predated that system, and became a surrogate talent-spotter at a time when very often it was a newspaper who broke the news of the progress of an eligible player to the FAI and not the other way around as it is now.

'Liam Tuohy was the youths coach then, and he always wanted to know how players were doing. He'd even be asking me if I'd seen any lines in the local papers about Irish guys scoring for the reserves or whatever. I also used to ring up the FAI with any information I had. You've got to remember the lines of communication were bad and there were very little resources in Merrion Square then.

'I would ring players up who had come across to a club here. I would enquire of them about their age, and whether they had been capped or not. They'd usually tell me that they didn't know if the FAI knew they were Irish or not. And these were lads who'd come over. But we're talking about days when the FAI didn't have a telex machine. I remember a youths squad being named once which had three players in it, two of whom were no longer in the game and the other of which had a broken leg. This was crazy stuff.

'I was involved in tipping them off about a few players – Terry Phelan, I suppose, was one. I don't think anybody knew that he was one of ours until I pointed him out, and then there was Mick McCarthy. Shortly before he left Barnsley for Manchester City, I did a piece like, you know, "I'd love to play for Ireland, says Mick," and two weeks later, Eoin Hand included him in the squad for the first time ever, and he was there for the great years and went on to become the manager.'

Hennessy witnessed the glory years but it was the barren ones that preceded them which left more of an impression. 'In those days, the international manager didn't have the support network that exists now. At the time, Eoin Hand used to go to Highbury on the Saturday before internationals and commandeer a room as a base for communication. From there, he'd find out who's available and who got crocked. I can remember driving home from racing meetings, listening to BBC Sports Report; I'd hear that Kevin O'Callaghan got crocked and I would try to contact Terry Conroy to tell Hand this because the team might be travelling out the next day.'

The Hand era may ultimately have ended in disappointment but Hennessy has good memories of the time. When the Irish team travel abroad now, there is usually a phalanx of media in tow. Back then, there would be at most half a dozen reporters at an away game and there were few barriers between them and the players. Hennessy recalls a famous night in Reykyavik when he accompanied Hand to a party at the Icelandic manager's house. One of his photographs of the evening shows the two managers sitting on a couch watching the Irish captain Tony Grealish playing the spoons on his knee. It was a less formal, more relaxed era.

'We were playing a qualifier in Malta and a pal of mine who lived there had tipped me off about problems with the ground. I went down, and the ground staff were on strike. I got the story for *The Sunday Press* that there were still pipes, nuts, bolts and bricks on the pitch, 24 hours before the game. The news broke and the Arsenal and Liverpool players were on to their clubs who were telling them not to play. Anyway, the FAI call this press conference where they put these rocks they had picked up on the pitch on the table, and asked me to take the photographs. I acted as the official photographer and clicked away with my little brownie camera.'

It wasn't all jollity at international level. Shortly after Jack Charlton succeeded Hand, Hennessy was present on the fateful night in Leeds when the new manager undermined Liam Tuohy to such an extent that he resigned as youths coach. Up to then, Tuohy had led Irish youths teams to three European Championships and a World Cup. 'I have this photograph, a great shot of Noel O'Reilly and Brian Kerr pulling the skips out of the dressing-room and in the corner, there was Man U representatives speaking with Derek Brazil. I had another photo of Tuohy holding a training session, the last picture of him training an Irish squad before he handed in his resignation. I never realised at the time how historic a picture that was going to be.'

Kerr and O'Reilly went back to working in the League of Ireland until they came back into the youths structure at the beginning of 1997. The first 18 months of their stewardship have been the most successful in the history of young Irish teams. When Kerr and O'Reilly were leading their Under-16 to become the first Irish team to win a European championship in May 1998, Hennessy sent a good luck fax. 'I just wrote about how sad the years we've lost are, how irretrievably gone without any progression whatsoever.'

The National Union of Journalists has a rule stating that any of its members who furnishes a colleague with a phone number of a contact is entitled to payment. When the Irish papers come calling, those he works for and those he doesn't, Hennessy never charges them a penny for the number of whichever footballer they are looking for. Even though it's become harder and harder for a freelance journalist to get stories published in an era when the daily papers often take an entire page of syndicated soccer from English publications, Hennessy will take no money for numbers. Goodwill means a lot to him. It is his trademark and the players he deals with know as much.

After the Hillsborough disaster in 1989, Kenny Dalglish imposed an immediate ban on any of his players speaking to the media. '*The Irish Independent* rang me and told me I had to get somebody. In the end, I got Ronnie Whelan at eight in the morning, and close to tears, he told me how, because he was the captain, the referee came over to him and said: "Get the players off." Then he gave me this story about how they were bouncing this ball around the dressing-room, wondering whether they were going back out when they heard there was one dead. Then they were wondering should they stay in when they heard there was more than one. He spoke all about the hurt he was feeling and it got trailed on the front of the *Evening Herald*. The first Liverpool player to speak after Hillsborough spoke to me. These are the little things that you cherish.'

Much like Gary Waddock, Whelan would have known and trusted Hennessy. Many years earlier the Liverpool player had travelled to London to link up with an Irish youths squad to discover the FAI hadn't booked him any accommodation and he spent the night at the Hennessy family home. At least Whelan found a bed: another player travelling on that same trip had to sleep overnight in the departure lounge of Heathrow. A life in the thrall of Irish soccer has provided Hennessy with a fund of such stories.

'You discover the funniest things when you ring up the digs and the landlady answers the phone. I rang this lady once and she said. "The Irish boy? Was that the one who never flushed the toilet? He's gone, he's moved somewhere else." But it works the other way too. I rang an apprentice at a club in the Midlands one time who told me that his Polish landlady had plonked a Kitkat down on his plate on the Sunday and told him that was his tea. The poor lad wanted to know what he should do about it.

'It can be tough for boys to cope with things like that but the problem is that I've known a lot of players who've had one foot in O'Connell Street and one over here. I always recommend it to them like this. I say: "You've been given a chance that the majority of guys would give their right arms for and for God's sake, grab it, forget about your mates back in Dublin. Get in ten years here, make a good career for yourself, be sensible with your money and set yourself up for life." '

In the time that Hennessy has been covering the game, English soccer has changed immeasurably. A favourite method of getting players' numbers used to be doorstepping them before they got back on the team coach to go home. In an age of high security, this isn't as straightforward a technique as it used to be. With the tabloids seemingly awash with money, he likes to boast that only one Irish player ever asked him for a fee for an interview. Needless to say, he didn't pay.

Having left PA in 1990, Hennessy's now entirely freelance, and can't afford to attend as many away games as he used to. Usually he just makes do with taking his son to see the live transmission at the Irish centre in Reading. However, last September, *Morgunbladdid* paid for him to travel to Reykyavik for Ireland v Iceland. He was also invited to speak at a pre-match function for Iceland's 100 club, a group of patrons who in return for a yearly financial stipend get the privilege of the team manager explaining his selection to them one hour before kick-off. After Hennessy delivered a speech peppered with stories about Jack Charlton, he was besieged by well-wishing locals.

'They kept coming up to me, telling me that all those years they were reading the paper, they thought it was a made-up byline. They were delighted to see I was real.' Several generations of Irish footballers would most likely agree.

Chapter Eight

Saints alive

*'Success is measured not so much by the position that
we have reached as by the obstacles that have been
overcome.'*
SIGN ON THE WALL IN ST. PATRICK'S ATHLETIC FC

Standing just inside the entrance to a National League of
Ireland club on a Saturday evening in April 1997, the club
secretary answered the enquiry about the expected gate
with a hopeful air: 'Maybe 100'. Talking to him again, two
and a half hours later, he was more exact. 'Thirty-eight paid
in'.

The anecdote is not meant as a cheap criticism of the
league but merely an illustration of its problems. In Dublin
city, derby games have attracted something in the region of
6-8,000 on a regular basis in the last couple of seasons and
even in Cork, the odd glamour fixture can push the figure
over the 5,000 mark, but these are exceptions. The rule is
much different.

On average, one National League club a year runs into
such financial trouble that its very existence is threatened.
We're not talking about just the small clubs here either. This
past decade, Cork, Dundalk, Derry City, and Galway United,
all population centres with palpable soccer traditions, have

flirted with extinction because of bad management, stadium trouble, spiralling wages and most common of all, falling crowds.

The majority of National League clubs are not supported in numbers sufficient to make them viable. Profitability generally doesn't even come into it. Home Farm FC, the adult wing of the esteemed schoolboy club, only began paying their players in 1995, yet within two years, they had an annual wage bill of £175,000 compared to gate receipts of £16,000.

For long spells, the National League has remained untouched by the boom which the success of the international team brought to soccer in Ireland. Those people who suddenly became interested in the game were more taken by the cross-channel fixtures than those going on up the road. Even still, critics of the League maintain that there are almost as many fans flying to games in England each week as there are attending domestic fixtures.

Whatever may be the case, the League has definitely struggled to shake off its negative public image as a structure which plays host to too many shysters, conmen and fly-by-nights. To some it will always be a dreadfully marketed entity distinguished only by primitive toilet facilities and poor quality football. More corrugated iron than corporate box.

The denizens of St Patrick's Athletic would beg to differ. To them the National League is flawed, certainly, but it also has potential that has been largely untapped. With the proper commitment and hard work, these people feel that the League can become more an object of admiration and less a subject of ridicule. The journey this club has made, from the brink of extinction to sell-out crowds, awesome merchandising and marketing, and a grip on the fanaticism of thousands in their hinterland should be a lesson to us all.

'Winners are workers. Losers make excuses.' The poster-sized epigrams on the wall of the home team dressing-room seem to inform the thinking of everybody at the club. The clock has not yet ticked past eight in the morning, and the offices are alive with the hum of activity. Pat Dolan, the manager and chief executive, has already been at his desk for over half an hour. Sitting in his swivel chair, on the phone, he has the voice of Tim O'Flaherty, the chairman, in one ear while the other is cocked to the prices being listed for him by Phil O'Farrell, the kit manager. An hour before the rest of the world opens for business, Saint Patrick's Athletic are trying to turn an honest buck.

Dolan is mentally computing the potential mark-up on merchandise being shown to him by O'Farrell. In their desire to stock the club shop with the best items available, they have received samples from sources as diverse as Belgium and the US. The key-rings and pennants they're thinking of ordering have to make a decent return but they can't be priced out of the reach of their fans. It's a dilemma, but only of the kind that a successful concern thrives on. That Dolan and O'Farrell are sitting here at all discussing which size pennant their fans would prefer to hang from their car mirrors is one more testimony to how far they've travelled.

Four years ago, St Patrick's Athletic played their home games in a rented dog-track in Harold's Cross, and plastered Dublin city with baffling posters about their seemingly forever imminent return to Richmond Park. These days, Richmond Park is frequently referred to as 'The Stadium of Light'. A somewhat overblown description of a facility which boasts seating on only one side, certainly, but another barometer of the progress they have made into people's imaginations.

The office, which at this early hour plays host to several club officials, is a story in itself. When Pat Dolan joined the club in 1992, this room was closed-off and out of bounds, a part of the building that was reckoned derelict. Back then, the actual office was a room downstairs in which a fireplace and a single lightbulb were the only sop to furniture. Dolan was appalled at what he found. The title of player-commercial manager sounded a lot less appetising when he didn't even have a chair to offer visitors. He cadged a desk from somewhere, before bartering two season tickets for wallpaper, carpet and the installation of electricity. Nothing too plush but a start all the same.

In those days, the current chairman was just another fan, albeit one with a long memory. Tim O'Flaherty had been supporting St Pat's since the '50s, a golden age in League of Ireland history. His folk memory stretched back to a famous cup match in Dundalk where St Pat's were wrongfully denied a certain goal, and a riot of sorts ensued. The decades since that infamous incident had been kinder to O'Flaherty than St Pat's. As he built up a hugely successful business, Liberty Air Technology, his favourite club lurched from one crisis to another. Seeing their obvious distress and wondering if he could help out, he left his business card with Dolan and the then team manager, Brian Kerr.

'I remember sitting in the Leinster House pub one night with Brian and the two of us were saying: "What are we going to do next? We're breaking our balls and making no progress." Then we discovered that this guy, Tim O'Flaherty, had given us both his business card so we reckoned he was worth a shot. I cycled up to his office. I only had a bicycle at the time and I was trying so hard to give off the image of a smooth businessman that I hid the bike around the corner so that he couldn't see it. He gave me £650, and I was trying to play it really cool but that money was going to make my life so much easier. It was beautiful.'

From there, O'Flaherty expanded his interest to become first a committee member and then chairman. It was at his behest that Dolan was given the title of chief executive, and it's been under the stewardship of them both that St Pat's have forged ahead of their rivals to become the most progressive outfit in the National League. The bicycle is just a funny story now; Dolan recently took delivery of his new company car, a Volvo.

Above the fireplace in his office, there hangs a mirror bearing an image of the club logo emerging from a bed of flames. 'The phoenix from the flames, that's us,' says Dolan. Around the crest, the motto spelt out in Irish reads: *Ni ceart go cur le cheile*. There is no strength without unity. Under the circumstances, it seems mighty apt.

In the 1960s, The Galtee Mor dancehall in Cricklewood, north London, was a meeting point for the young Irish abroad in the city. Forced to leave their families and homes in the search for gainful employment, the emigrants sought solace there at weekends among their own people. In a foreign land, it was a comforting place where the sing-song sounds of familiar accents might take the edge off a gnawing loneliness. The Galtee Mor, and its equivalents like The National in Kilburn were more than dancehalls. They were part of the ad hoc expatriate community support network, and in time, they became renowned as venues which spawned thousands of Irish marriages.

Vincent Dolan and Maryjoe Doherty fit the stereotype nicely. He was an engineer from Ardrahan, county Galway; she was a nurse from Carndonagh, county Donegal. Their romance, which took its first tentative steps at the Galtee Mor, blossomed after Maryjo had come back to work in Galway and eventually they married. On 20 September 1967, Maryjo gave birth to twin boys, Eamonn and Pat. Vincent's career eventually took them back to England where he began working for the Ford motor company at their research and design facility at Denton. The Dolans settled in the country town of Chelmsford, Essex where their children grew up with English accents framed by very Irish sensibilities.

'My Irishness is not something I'm conscious of or that I have control over. It's not contrived like it can be with some Americans. I have no control over this at all, it's in my heart. We spent five weeks every summer back in Carndonagh, and that part of the world has such special memories for me. I'm very proud too of being a Galway man.'

The reminiscences of his childhood bear him out. In the Essex playground where he and his brother honed their soccer skills, the games invariably took place between West Ham United and Galway Rovers. On Sunday afternoons, Vincent Dolan would take his boys out in the car, and drive to the top of the nearest hill. There, he would fiddle with the car aerial until such time as a listenable signal was attained and the Dolan boys could hear RTE's live sports programme. They'd hang on every word of the Gaelic football or hurling commentary and wait impatiently for the Galway Rovers result to be announced. One of his most enduring memories is of the late Belgian goal that denied Eoin Hand's team World Cup qualification in 1981.

The Dolans' interest in sport was matched only by their ability and Pat was proficient enough to represent Essex Under-14s at soccer, cricket and rugby. 'Being talented at sport is a huge advantage in life when you're growing up. Once you start playing football well, it makes you more attractive to women and it becomes a talking point. People start to give you respect.'

None more so than the scouts from the big London clubs who came courting the Dolans with offers. Eamonn went to Upton Park, where his progress was such that one year he was voted 'Young Hammer of the Year', ahead of the second-placed Paul Ince. His career was finally ended by testicular cancer. West Ham was also an option for Pat but he had already been seduced by Arsenal.

'I went along to Arsenal, and there was a sense of tradition and history about the place that appealed to me. When you walked up to Highbury, there was a sign there that said: "The home of football". I thought: "yeah, that'll do me." '

Signing for Arsenal meant leaving school early. At the King George VI grammar school, an establishment which boasted the highest number of Oxbridge candidates outside the public schools, this was not the done thing. Pat Dolan had been one of the youngest prefects ever there, and the headmaster was not best pleased to see him depart after gaining 11 'O'levels. 'He called me in and he said [putting on a plum accent], "Tell me Dolan, do you think you can make a living from this football?" '

At Highbury, everything pointed to the fact that the people who mattered believed he could. Dolan captained the youth team, became the youngest PFA (Professional Footballers' Association) representative ever, and even had a spell coaching the club's Under-16s. Off the field, he and the other apprentices received tutoring from Kate Hoey, who would later become a Labour Party MP, while on the field, international recognition came quickly. At the age of 17, the Dolan brothers were called up en bloc for an Irish youths game against Northern Ireland. Pat broke his leg and missed the match, Eamonn marked his début with a hat-trick.

'The first game I was involved in was against England at Tolka Park. There were 12,000 people there, and I think it was the first time we'd ever beaten them at that level, and I still remember the way I felt that night. It was just such a wonderful feeling. Myself and Niall Quinn came back to training at Arsenal on the Friday and we were buzzing. We'd beaten England, and they had Michael Thomas and Tony Adams who were also at the club. Boy, did we give them stick.

'I remember too, though, how disorganised the FAI were at the time. The English team were staying in Jury's and we were in the North Star hotel in Amiens Street. I was sharing a tiny room that had no bathroom in it. Then, Noel O'Reilly would arrive to bring us out to training in Belfield in a car or a van. No team bus, nothing.'

It is difficult for Dolan to tell a story like that without lapsing into a discussion on the present state of Irish soccer. You sense it is never far from his mind. 'How times have changed in that respect, and that's good because they should have. At the time, players were treated very poorly, and if you don't have the aspiration to provide first class facilities for your players, you're going nowhere. That's what's wrong with Irish soccer now. We don't have first class anything now but that doesn't mean we shouldn't try to get it. When you say things like that, it makes you unpopular especially if the people you are saying it to are all younger than you.'

At international level, Dolan's singular devotion to the cause marked him out. Bob Hennessy, a freelance journalist who covered almost all the youth and Under-21 internationals of the period remembers. 'Patrick was captain of the team, and we'd lost to Scotland in a Euro qualifier and this was a game we needed to win to go through to the tournament itself. After the match, I went back to the team hotel, I'm walking up the stairs and I see the door to one of the rooms open, and inside sitting on the bed, there's Patrick visibly crying. It meant that much to him.'

During that period, Arsenal was perceived within the game as being a club with a discipline problem. As they fished around for a manager in 1986, speculation was that the position would go to George Graham, a distinguished old boy with a no-nonsense reputation. 'After Don Howe resigned,' says Dolan, 'I saw George Graham at a match at Highbury, and I actually held the door open for him, and I thought to myself: "I really hope he gets the job. He's a disciplinarian, he'll sort this club out." I was thinking, somebody like me, who trains hard and doesn't mess around will do well under George Graham. Ten years ago, I was going on about diet and the importance of looking after the body and they all laughed at me. Now Dennis Bergkamp says it and they're all into it.'

Graham eventually arrived but contrary to what he had initially hoped, Dolan was not one of those favoured by the new manager. He has his own theory as to why. 'We were playing an FA youths cup match against Millwall, and things weren't going our way. So Pat Rice was the coach, and he starts shouting at me. I just shouted back "Fuck off!". George Graham was still in charge of Millwall then and he was at the game. Because of that one incident I think he saw me as undisciplined and part of the attitude problem.' Arsenal released Pat Dolan at the age of 20.

'After Arsenal, I didn't want to play for anybody. I found it very difficult to come to terms with the fact that they didn't consider me good enough to play for them, and I didn't want to play for anybody else in the UK game. I wanted to come and play at the highest level in my own country. I look back on my time at Arsenal as invaluable. It was a fantastic grounding and it had a profound influence on my life. But if I was playing for Arsenal today, I wouldn't be doing what I'm doing now with St Patrick's Athletic. If somebody asked me now, who would I rather manage, Arsenal or St Pat's, there would be no competition. St Pat's every time.'

Following an unhappy spell at Walsall, which included a loan period at St Pat's, Dolan signed for Galway United in the summer of 1990. In an interview in an Arsenal match programme years earlier, he had been asked which other club he'd like to play for. He answered: 'Galway Rovers'. When he made his début for Galway United, as they had become, somebody brought along the old programme. 'It was a dream come true. My first game was against Dundalk who were the champions, and we ended up winning 1-0. It was everything I'd hoped it would be.'

Unfortunately, from that point on, Galway United only lived down to his expectations. At the end of his first season he departed, aggrieved at the way he felt that the manager Paul McGee was being unfairly treated by the directors. 'I told the directors "you're never going to win anything with that attitude." Lo and behold, I got to the FAI Cup final the next year with Shamrock Rovers and we ended up losing to Galway. A lot of those Galway players were still my mates so I went back to the Burlington Hotel with them afterwards, and I had to face all those directors I'd told off.'

Dolan's introduction to the politicking of the League was only beginning. After one season with Rovers, he found himself taking on the dual role of player-commercial manager of St Pat's. On his 22nd birthday, he met John Bale, the owner of the club at the Westbury Hotel off Grafton Street. Bale, who was by reputation a millionaire, arrived at the meeting wearing odd shoes and driving a Fiat Uno. A surreal evening ensued in the company of Bale, George Best and Eamon Dunphy, the proceedings culminating in a £400 champagne bill being paid out of club coffers, and an appearance on *The Late Late Show*.

The splurging of club funds on champagne didn't quite fit the reality of what Dolan encountered at Inchicore. Apart from the dreadful condition of the club office, there was the little matter of the dressing-room showers. 'The showers would never work. You had to fill up the tank with a hose pipe, and if you didn't get into the showers in the first five minutes, there was just a little trickle, nothing else. This was how the club was run and when I first came to the club, I enjoyed the romance of it all but then I decided this isn't right. We must be more professional.'

A minor detail maybe, but these days the dressing-rooms at Richmond Park epitomise what he means. 'When I signed for Galway United, there wasn't even a toilet in the dressing-room. I complained and they told me it was the players' own responsibility. If you go to Highbury you'll see that there are four toilets in the dressing-room and if it's good enough for Arsenal football club, it's good enough for St Pat's. That's what we measure ourselves against'.

The road from profligacy to professionalism and decent toilets was long and hard. For one six-month period, the players received no wages and more than once, Dolan was forced to dip into his savings to keep the squad happy at the end of a week. Through a succession of directors and even owners, some were more committed than others. Richard Black did great work on behalf of the club and Phil Mooney, a Pat's official for 20 years continues to be a stalwart as a director. Then there's O'Flaherty, the man Dolan credits with 'taking it to the next level'.

'If it's not the most important thing in people's lives, they should not be at this club. We found that out the hard way. Committee members who don't go to away games shouldn't be involved with us. What kind of message does it send to the players and the fans if a director can't be bothered to go? This club belongs to nobody except the people of west Dublin, and we are really only at the embryo stage. Potentially, there are 500,000 people in our constituency and only with full commitment can we get those people in.'

When he started out on this adventure, people used to tell Dolan that he'd never get youngsters supporting St Pat's ahead of Liverpool and Manchester United. He begged to differ, and found others of a similar mind. Outside the home team dressing-room, a plaque near the door reads: 'Conor O'Dowd, never forgotten, never replaced. Come on you Supersaints.'

Dolan explains: 'Conor was a leader, the greatest young man you could meet. People used to say to me, "you'll never get young people supporting St Pat's" but Conor and his friends epitomised the Supersaints mentality, the new breed. He was Irish and he wanted to support an Irish club, the same as if he was from Paraguay, he'd support a Paraguayan club. Suddenly, he was out there playing with his brother Tony, and he got a heart attack. He was absolutely marvellous and he was just taken away. It was a hammer blow to this club.'

The 'Supersaints' motif is Dolan's favourite brainchild. 'All these little things, you say them and then you start believing them. "Saintmania" was the term we coined first. Then people said, "You're a maniac, you can't do that." I said: "Well, I've already gone ahead and done it." Next up was the programme and I decided I was going to call it "The Supersaint". They told me I couldn't but I'd already went ahead and did it. They told me that the "Supersaints" idea would never work, and it's been a phenomenal success for us. So many people actually call us the "Supersaints" now.'

His eye for the marketing initiative is reflected in the calibre of companies which take perimeter advertising at the ground. Alongside local concerns, there are global brands like Zanussi, Canon, Amstel and Burger King. Standing alongside him in the centre-circle one afternoon as he tried to sell hoarding space to the man from Nissan Ireland, it was revealing how, for the hard sell, the man in the three piece suit reverted to the man in the tracksuit. 'Eddie Gormley is one of the best dead ball kickers in the league, right, and he takes all our inswinging corners from there, and (turning quickly) there. We score a huge percentage of goals from his corners, so sites by those corner flags would be very advantageous in terms of TV highlights exposure.'

The array of multi-national names is impressive but the canvassing of the local business community has been even more central to the club's renaissance. For the last couple of years, their jersey sponsors have been Autoglass, the Irish arm of the same company which endorses Chelsea. The relationship has blossomed to the extent that the Managing Director, Phil Egan, is somebody who Dolan often asks advice of on business matters. 'Why shouldn't I ask him?

That guy is the market leader in his field, he's bound to be able to help me improve our club.'

Dolan can claim market leadership too. When he calls the club programme, 'our Matchday magazine, the best ever in Irish football,' he says it all without flinching because he knows it's undeniably true. The programme is a lucrative venture, made more so by the way in which it is produced inhouse by the commercial manager, Michael Glynn, and the media officer, Gary Brannigan. The quality would put many FA Premiership clubs to shame, and since the advertising revenue alone covers the printing cost, every magazine sold represents a profit.

There are few clubs who can make such boasts. Then again, there are few National League clubs as well run as this one. St Pat's make more in selling gold club season tickets in the stand at £250 a go than some of their rivals make in gate receipts for a season. In the 1997/98 campaign, the full house sign was used regularly at Richmond Park. It may be true that a bit of success attracts support but walk into any shop or pub in the hinterland of Richmond Park, and a poster advertising St Pat's next home fixture will stare back at you. The extent of support they receive is not by accident but design.

On the Tuesday morning that we meet, the Irish tabloids are full of the exploits of the Newcastle United players on the streets of Dublin. 'Gilly was out cold, there was blood everywhere' screamed the headline in *The Star*. The misunderstanding with Alan Shearer which caused Keith Gillespie to visit the accident and emergency room of a Dublin hospital for stitches is relentlessly relayed to the journalists by eyewitnesses and passers-by. Sitting at his desk, Pat Dolan hasn't had time to read the papers yet but he knows the gist of the story.

A horrified facial expression prefaces his comments. 'That's just typical of what people are trying to import here in Dublin with Wimbledon. It's this Magaluf and Benidorm culture, lager-lout behaviour. When the Irish Under-20s went to Malaysia with Brian Kerr for the World Cup last year, they behaved impeccably all through. A credit to their country off the field, they reached the semi-finals on it. The behaviour of some of the England team, let's just say, left a lot to be desired.'

St Pat's have been in the vanguard of opposition towards the move to relocate Wimbledon to Dublin. When Clydebank also announced themselves as would be relocators to Dublin in February 1998, Dolan took the opportunity to tell one newspaper that his club had no intention of moving to either Scotland or London. Four months earlier, he had outlined his opposition to such proposals in an article which he wrote for *The Sunday Tribune*. As the most cogent critique against the putative Dublin Dons, it is worth reproducing in full.

'Wimbledonmania' has dominated some sections of the Irish media in an attempt to condition the Irish soccer public that whatever the ethical, moral or legal arguments against an English club abandoning their home to commercially exploit Ireland's love of sport, nothing or no-one could stop it.

The game of soccer is the most popular globally, purely because it transcends social background, sex, colour, creed, age or nationality. People, supporters, are the integral fabric of soccer. If advocates of this scheme put commercial gains ahead of people and supporters, what is the future for football?

If Wimbledon's new football visionaries simply wish to benefit from being Ireland's representatives in a European Super league, why not join the National League? A new National League club in Clondalkin in a 60,000 capacity stadium would be welcomed by St Pat's.

Many noble Irish soccer heroes such as Blanchflower, Tuohy, Giles and Best dreamed of an All Ireland team. With peace on our island now a realistic aspiration, already the feasibility of an All Ireland League is being discussed by clubs north and south of the border. Wimbledon in Ireland, playing in the English Premiership, would kill such a dream stone dead.

Employment opportunities, that for the first time in decades, are available to young Irish professional players, would suddenly be limited to players vying for 11 places on one team. Thomas Morgan captained Ireland to glorious success in Malaysia, where Irish players defied the odds and succeeded, coached and managed by Irish people.

Thomas Morgan, Trevor Molloy and Colin Hawkins are new Irish soccer heroes who want to live and work in Ireland with St Patrick's Athletic. St Pat's are an integral part of the social fabric of west Dublin: our schoolboy teams provide a secure and constructive environment for hundreds of youngsters. Wimbledon's arrival would undermine this vital role and damage the social fabric of community life nationwide.

What about that great English export, the soccer lout? Does Dublin want to encourage hooligans who will undoubtedly impact negatively on our economic prosperity and consume police, court and prison resources?

Our advice to Wimbledon's visionaries is to look elsewhere. Your scheme is morally, ethically and most crucially, legally wrong. For £2m or even £2bn, the Supersaints will never abandon the most important people in our football world – our supporters. Your future, our future, the future of Irish soccer is secure, as we will not allow Irish soccer to be destroyed for financial gain.

'Morgan, Molloy and Hawkins were three of the most prominent players on the Irish Under-20 team which, under the management of Brian Kerr, finished third in the World Cup in Malaysia. Dolan, who succeeded Kerr as Pat's team manager in January 1997, travelled halfway across the world for the latter stages of the competition and eventually signed up all three. Morgan and Hawkins, stars of the tournament, had been released by their English clubs, Blackburn Rovers and Coventry City, at the end of the 1996/97 season.

'Glamour is a perception, the reality is something different. People here are very naïve about what the professional game in England entails, how hard it is to go over there and survive. That's why we need a strong game here. I'm not saying for one minute that players shouldn't go to England to play. If it's the right thing for them and their careers they definitely should. The problem is that for all players, it has become the only *option. In that respect, we have failed the Irish public but we can change that.'*

The obsession with the English game torments Dolan but the Wimbledon proposal inflames him like nothing else. His commitment to stopping the move, however, doesn't blind him to the fact that domestic football (a term he despises) has got huge problems. 'I'm very proud to be part of an Irish soccer industry that at last has taken a long hard look at itself and said: "We're not good enough, we must change." But we need help. We need to give the Celtic Tiger time to bite into our soccer industry and we need help from the media, the politicians and from the FAI. I hope they will look at progressive clubs like us, clubs that have got up off their knees and not just got the begging bowl out. We have shown what can be done, and if people don't recognise that, they don't recognise an Irish success story. '

Dolan argues that Wimbledon could never connect with a community in Dublin like Pat's do. There's too much history, too much passion. An incident later in the day bears that out to some extent. As Dolan makes his way back to the office after lunch, his name is called from down the street, and three teenagers approach. 'Pat, we were wonderin' if you could give us some advice, we're tryin' to start a soccer club over in the flats,' they chorus. They have come to the right man, wearing the wrong clothes. 'You, take off that United hat,' he says, pointing at one offender. 'You (pointing at another), get rid of the Spurs scarf, and come back here in about an hour.'

Within an hour, the teenage locals seeking Dolan's counsel have dwindled in number from three to two, and divested themselves of their offending Premiership paraphernalia. Sitting in his office, they hand over a typed up proposal which they hope will gain them entry to the Dublin schoolboys' league. Immediately, he is won over to their cause: 'You want to call the team St Michael's Boys, well, you can be the Supersaints as well, can't you?' is his opening salvo.

Flicking through their plan, Dolan begins listing what

must be done next. 'We've got to get politicians on board, get a jersey made up, look at where you can get sponsorship . . . ' The boys, Anthony Piercey and Eddie Rogers, are visibly excited by what he is saying. At Friday night home games, they stand at The Shed end of Richmond Park. Pat Dolan, one of their heroes, has invited them into his office and is taking their dream on board. As they leave, he hands them two kit bags and a set of training cones as a keep-sake. 'I'll come over there to see you in a month, and if I see those cones being used properly, I'll know that you're serious about this. '

His visitors departed, he begins enthusing about a video made by a group from St Michael's Estate on the community. 'That estate has real problems with drugs and unemployment but the support of those people is very important to this club. Our first aim here is to produce a professional football club with a great ground that is good enough to successfully represent Ireland in Europe. But we also want to make a positive contribution to this community. By being here, we can affect people's lives for the better.'

From the balcony of his apartment above The Horse and Jockey pub in Inchicore, Dolan can make out the bare outlines of the training and main pitches at Richmond Park. 'My Dad was a huge Bill Nicholson fan, you know, and he used to live near White Hart Lane when he managed Spurs. I read somewhere that Bill Shankly lived right next to Anfield too. At the time that I moved in to this flat, I wasn't manager of St Pat's but I knew that I was on some sort of crusade to change this club.' Bill Shankly. Bill Nicholson. Obsessed, driven and successful men. Dolan is coming from the same place.

Over the past decade, the almost uniformly poor performances of Irish club teams in Europe have been a constant bugbear for the National League. Dolan is already working to ensure that when his team carry the Irish flag onto the continent, they will not fail for the wrong reasons. 'I think that too often our clubs have been inclined to go to the pub and press the excuse button about fitness. Well, fitness will not be our excuse. We will be as mentally and physically prepared as any Irish team in Europe ever has been. We may still lose games, we might come off second best, but no stone will have been left unturned. I can't accept failure when people haven't given their all.'

Twenty years before St Pat's, Shamrock Rovers were the last Irish club to go fully professional. At the time, their manager Johnny Giles made the grandiose claim that within seven years, he hoped his team would be capable of winning the European Cup. When the dream fell apart after four seasons, he was never allowed to forget that. Eamon Dunphy, now a central figure in the Wimbledon for Dublin consortium, then a player-coach with Giles at Rovers, sees similarities between the two clubs.

'I admire Pat Dolan for his guts, and for what he's trying to achieve,' says Dunphy. 'But our dream was doomed from the start because the infrastructure wasn't here to support what we were doing. We couldn't even get a proper gym to use, and if the weather was bad, we had to train in the car-park instead of on the grass. I think the infrastructure has improved but maybe not enough. It's no use one or two clubs striving for excellence when the rest are way behind. What Pat Dolan doesn't have to face is the hostility from officials that was there towards what we were doing.'

Twenty years after Giles and Dunphy talked of giddy nights in Europe, Shamrock Rovers are forced to shuttle between various Dublin venues to play their home games while scraping for planning permission to build a new stadium in Tallaght. Their famous old ground, Glenmalure Park, has long since been turned into a housing estate, the costly price of flawed romanticism.

St Pat's' pursuit of supreme fitness has seen the club adopt initiatives like constantly measuring the body fat of their 35 squad members. The players make extensive use of the state-of-the-art facilities in the Total Fitness complex in Blanchardstown, west Dublin, and their fitness training is co-ordinated by Dave Mahedy, a coach with a track record of excellence that crosses the sporting boundaries between gaelic games, soccer and rugby.

'Dave won the league and cup with Eoin Hand at Limerick but I first noticed him working with the Limerick hurlers that reached two All Ireland finals. Then I saw he was involved with the Munster rugby team when they were doing well. I thought to myself, this guy has the Midas touch. I've got to meet him.'

Based in Limerick, Mahedy didn't initially envisage driving up to Dublin twice a week for training but Dolan's enthusiasm got the better of him. One weekend this season, he flew back from Amsterdam for an away fixture in Ballybofey that was postponed an hour before kick-off. How quickly he was consumed.

Ask Dolan how many full-time professional players he has in his squad and he'll answer: 'They're all professional.' When you clarify that you're looking for the number who don't have another job, he admits to 12. You work out for yourself that his own and the club's creed is contained in the first answer.

'Football is a game of chance but you can limit the accidents. You have control over the medical and physical side of preparation and it's important that you don't leave any doors open. That is what being professional is all about and we are demanding standards of our players. They have to be fit, and there's tremendous togetherness in getting there.'

Speaking in the first week in March, Dolan was philosophical about whether Pat's or Shelbourne would prevail in the Premier League title race that had long since become a two-horse race. 'I have the youngest team in this country and the newest team in the country, and to even be in the position of challenging is great. I know how fickle football fans can be. When you're on top of the table, and you draw with Bohs and a supporter shouts: "You're only a schoolboy manager, Dolan," you realise how fickle this is, how fleeting. I'm just enjoying being up there.'

Dolan prefers to think of other moments in the campaign that have convinced him of the intrinsic worth of the job he's doing. 'After drawing a game against UCD (University College, Dublin), I was really down because we had played so badly. But driving through Inchicore afterwards, I saw these boys playing football in the street. Five of them were wearing St Pat's jerseys and the other had an Ireland top on. That cheered me up so much.'

The intensity that he brings to the task means that Dolan rarely stops working before midnight. His friends and fellow Supersaints are constantly on at him to look after himself better. They have seen how the svelte part-time model who began the job six years ago has evolved into somebody with a severe weight problem. To him, it is the price of his passion.

'I know that I will have to change eventually, and get a grip on my life. Physically, I've let myself go and my lifestyle doesn't help. I keep bad hours, I eat the wrong things and I do worry about the effects on my health. What do I say, though? I'm going off to look after myself and let Shels or Bohs or Rovers win the league. I can't walk away from this. Not now.'

On Friday, 1 May the last night of the season, St Patrick's Athletic won the Premier Division with a 2-1 victory away to Kilkenny City. Interviewed afterwards, Dolan dedicated the title win to 'the best supporters in the world' and Conor O'Dowd.

Chapter Nine

The man who puts
the boys in green

One Friday night in the autumn of 1996, Brian Kerr made a decision which even at a distance of less than two years can be judged one of the most fortuitous in the history of Irish soccer. Driving home after a St Patrick's Athletic match at Richmond Park, Kerr took a detour towards the Football Association of Ireland's head office at Merrion Square in Dublin city centre. He drove there with the thought of applying for the recently advertised position of Irish youths coach. Sitting in his car, he jotted down a letter, slipped it inside an envelope and popped it through the letter box. Although the official deadline for applications had been seven and a half hours previously at close of business, he thought there might still be time.

Ten years earlier, Kerr had been an integral part of the backroom team as Liam Tuohy, a former youths manager, took Ireland to the finals of three European championships and one World Cup before resigning on account of interference by Jack Charlton. Content with his lot as manager of St Patrick's Athletic, who were then National League champions, Kerr thought he could combine his club role with the part-time international position, and that notion comforted him as he drove off into the night and home.

But Kerr was mistaken about the job. The FAI wanted a full-time manager and by the beginning of January 1997, he had taken leave of absence from his work as a laboratory technician in UCD, resigned as manager of St Patrick's Athletic, and together with his assistant, Noel O'Reilly, embarked on a run of success so unprecedented that it has become almost routine for his teams to return from abroad to official government receptions. In July 1997, his Irish Under-20 team finished third in the World Cup in Malaysia, at that time the highest ranking any team from Ireland had ever attained. A month later, he managed the Under-18s to fourth place in the European Championships in Iceland.

This season has been different only in that he has upped the ante further. In April, a new batch of Under-18s won the prestigious four-team Oporto tournament involving France, Portugal and Austria. A fine achievement in its own right, it paled against what came next. On Friday, 8 May 1998, the Irish Under-16s defeated Italy 2-1 at McDiarmaid Park in Perth to become European champions. They were the first Irish soccer team to win a major trophy at any level, and almost half a million people watched the game live on RTE.

Interviewed afterwards, Kerr paid fulsome tributes to many people, from the great to the good. 'I think [Liam] Tuohy would be a happy man tonight,' he said of his former mentor. 'I haven't talked to him but I don't need to. He's the master, he's like the grand master in chess. No, I don't need to talk to him tonight.'

Tuohy wasn't alone in attracting the plaudits as Kerr magnanimously deflected the glory from himself onto the game that spawned him. 'This is a win that a lot of people can be proud of. The ones who have worked in schoolboy football over the last 60 or 70 years with little or no reward, putting up nets, giving people lifts, managing and coaching teams. I hope that they too feel a part of this win in their hearts.'

The sentiment was expressed with the simple modesty that marks out a man, who even at the height of his current wave of glory, is always eager to play down his own personal input. 'I know there are lots of fellas who didn't get

169

the breaks and the opportunities that I got. I was fortunate that through the teams that I played for and managed, I met people who saw that from a young age I had a bit of madness about me for running teams. They saw I had the dedication and attention to detail even at that stage and I was lucky.

'Noel O'Reilly had an ability that maybe would have been spotted anyway. When Johnny Giles was trying the full-time thing with Shamrock Rovers in the 1970s, Noel was doing the training with them. I was working in Belfield and I used to be looking out the window watching Noel conducting the training so he had a great education there. But we have been fortunate. There might be loads of blokes around like us who've never got those breaks to go into the next level. There probably is a lot of fellas like us around.'

Utterly gracious towards his contemporaries in the Irish game, Kerr's own talent has already been noted by his fellow coaches from all around Europe. At a conference in Brussels last December, he gave a talk about Ireland's Malaysian campaign to a room full of other international youths managers. So impressive was his presentation that it was later voted best of the week. One more accolade in a football life that is speckled with them.

Frank and Margaret Kerr both hailed from Belfast but they brought up their five children in Drimnagh, a suburb of west Dublin. Brian, the youngest of their brood, was born in 1953 and spent his formative years immersed in sport. His father had been a good enough boxer to be champion of Ireland seven times, and the young Brian spent a lot of his childhood accompanying his father to the National Stadium, and soldiering with him on late night vigils watching the big fights from America on television.

For all that, Frank never pushed his son towards the ring, and Brian's instincts took him in another sporting direction. From the age of eight, he would trundle along to Richmond Park to see St Patrick's Athletic, but if soccer fired his dreams most, he wasn't averse to turning his hands to other sports. At school, he played Gaelic football to such a standard that he was captain of the team one season, and hurling caught his eye too, although his main talent at that game seems to have been less with the hurley and more with using his left foot to poach goals.

Eamonn Coghlan, with whom he grew up, was a good friend, and they often played soccer together for Rialto on Saturdays before running cross-country races on Sundays. By the age of 15, however, soccer matches also fell on a Sunday, and their career paths diverged. Coghlan went on to win an athletics scholarship to Villanova University which would lead him to international greatness while Kerr took his first steps along football's learning curve, setting off an a journey through the game which in time would be cited as evidence that the ultimate dream can still come true; that it is possible to go from managing teams every Saturday morning in local street leagues to being heavily tipped as the next likely Irish senior manager.

As a 15-year-old, Kerr was managing the Crumlin United under-13 team, and already management had got under his skin. 'I got a lot of pleasure out of running teams from the start. I loved organising the teams and finding the way over problems. Where people would say "you can't do that", I'd say "you can", and I liked confronting that. Kerr had been a talented enough player to make it into League of Ireland B with Shelbourne, and to secure an FAI Intermediate Cup medal with Bluebell United in 1982, but from the start it was apparent that his real gifts lay on the other side of the white lines.

His eye for the unlikely solution soon distinguished him from his contemporaries, and he was only 20 when Liam Tuohy appointed him manager of the Shamrock Rovers youth team. 'He was very good at man-management even when he was young,' says Tuohy. 'He's able to criticise a player and not lose their respect. He'll have a go and then it's forgotten. People say he can have a lovely disposition and be a narky whore at the same time.'

When Tuohy left Rovers for Shelbourne, he brought Kerr along as his assistant and though Tuohy left shortly after arriving, Kerr stayed on to manage the club's B team to runners-up spot in the league. After that, he spent two years with Mick Lawlor at Home Farm, and six months with the same man at Drogheda before being offered the manager's job at St Pat's. Along the way, Tuohy had enlisted Kerr as one of his trusted lieutenants with the Irish youths team. The learning process continued apace.

'I think that everybody who's ever had contact with Tuohy in football would feel that they owe him something. The five years that me and Noel had with him were the most educational but they were also the best times that I had in football. It was great because we were beating very good teams. On a very limited budget with very limited resources, we had success. We beat Portugal one time 3-2 and they had Paulo Futre up front. He'd just played 40 first team games for Sporting Lisbon and our two centre-backs, Noel Bollard and Shay Purcell, were playing for Cherry Orchard in the Dublin Schoolboys' League.'

The delight he takes in putting one over the so-called big name countries seems to sustain him to this day. 'When we're playing trial matches up in the AUL (Athletic Union Leauge) complex in the muck, I'd be looking at the pitch, and Noel would say "this gives us a chance, when we'll be playing France and Portugal, their blokes won't be used to this, the wind and the rain and the muck." And he's right, those conditions bring out something. It's a great learning ground for our fellas.

'You can be sure that in a lot of those other countries, the boys would be going out on lovely manicured pitches, and playing in schools of excellence from the age of 13, whereas our boys would be used to playing on the side of a hill with long grass and dirt where they have to muck in. That's a good thing because it's definitely character building.'

If the Tuohy years with Ireland were hallmarked by a lack of resources, there was always a surfeit of enthusiasm. The work was voluntary and in the absence of money for team buses, the coaching staff would often use their own cars to ferry players around to training. Nobody complained because they were enjoying the ride and learned so much as they went.

'I remember we were going to training one day in some far-flung spot, I think it was Iceland, and I was sitting with Noel saying "I wonder what he'll want us to do today." So Noel told me to ask him. "Liam," says I. "What do you want us to do this morning?" He says: "What the hell did I bring youse here for? Do whatever you want to do, I'm only here to watch the matches and pick the teams."

'That was the way, he'd let you get on with it and let it happen. Sometimes he'd ask you what you thought about the team and you'd tell him. Here was a man who had been Irish international manager asking a young fella like me what I thought and who should play. It was brilliant.'

The good times with Ireland ended when Jack Charlton strode unceremoniously into the youths' dressing room at half-time during a 1986 game against England at Elland Road, and undermined Tuohy's authority to the extent that he resigned his post. Charlton subsequently met with Kerr and O'Reilly, asking them to stay on, but those who know them both say they are men of honour and it wouldn't have fitted their way of doing things to remain involved with somebody who had slighted their boss in such a dreadful fashion.

'Tuohy was basically lost to the game out of bitterness, and he didn't deserve that. There was one fella who never made money out of the game and he was the most generous man with his time. He was always so helpful to everybody in the game and yet he was isolated and kept out of the game. There's people who have to look at themselves in relation to that, and ask themselves why.'

For his part, Kerr concentrated all his powers on managing St Pat's and when it came to international fixtures, he became involved in the same unseemly scramble for tickets as everybody else. He travelled to Italy in 1990 and the US in 1994 as an Irish supporter on package deals. He might not have been the biggest fan of the Charlton regime but he saw the pleasure it was bringing to millions.

'I enjoyed watching the joy people were feeling, I saw them getting a little bit of what I had every week watching and managing St Pat's. I enjoyed watching a lot of the officials get their reward with the trips. The officials normally get a bit of stick about being the knife and fork brigade and the blazers but I understood how much these people organise matches, leagues and referees. I could see that a lot of the officials were schoolboy and junior soccer men who had come through to the senior council. Now they might lack in other things, but they didn't lack in enthusiasm for the game.

'It didn't bother me looking in from the outside because I was enjoying what we were doing with Pat's. But I did feel upset that nobody wanted to come and see what we were doing, that the international manager never came to see Pat's playing. Or that the youths manager never came to see us. It wasn't as if I wanted him to come and say "youse were great" but he could have come and said "not bad, your team is well-organised, the centre-half is not bad". But not to *ever* come, that's bad.

'Up in the north, Billy Bingham and Bryan Hamilton at least went to the games. Now they might have thought the league up there wasn't up to much but they never said that, which at least gave some encouragement. What we got was a dig in the head and your neck twisted. That bothered me, it hurt me. And I think if everybody involved in League of Ireland at the time was honest, they'd say they were hurt too. I had no relationship with the international team, it was nothing to do with what I was doing at Pat's.'

Kerr spent ten years at St Patrick's Athletic, during which time they won the league twice. The first of those successes, which came in 1990, bridged a gap of 33 years to their last triumph. The way in which the victory was achieved that season points to much in Kerr's style of management. Denied the sort of money required to buy in a championship-winning team, he forged one by blending youth and experience. Six months after the second equally-remarkable title win in 1996, Kerr took his leave of Richmond Park for the Irish job.

'We'd finally got round to the stage where we had three or four exceptional people in there. It takes a long time to get that into a football club and it was great. This was a special group of top people with dedication and practical ability. There was a lovely balance; the calmness and ambassadorial ability of the director, Phil Mooney; the chairman, Tim O'Flaherty's business acumen and decisiveness; Pat Dolan's unique enthusiasm and workaholic nature. And maybe my abrasiveness and experience.

'By leaving, I felt that I was breaking up something very special and it was a huge decision. But they were very good and honourable about it. They knew I wanted to give the international thing a go, and my hands were tied because the FAI wanted it to be full-time. I feared a little bit for Pat's but I felt happy there was a good structure there. And the club have moved on from there since, and they have nearly a full-time set-up going in just over a year.'

Throughout his career, every team that Brian Kerr had been involved with had won more matches and finished higher in the league after he came along than they did before him. In an international sphere, he felt it might be a little difficult to keep that record up but if the essential goal was still the same, there were plenty of other overriding concerns too.

'I wanted to do it in a way that fellas were going to know someone was interested, that fellas were going to be picked fairly, without any hang-ups about where they came from, without any bias because of the club they were playing for. I was going to do my best to get the best team out for every match, and hopefully prepare them to win matches, and to think that they were going to win matches. And I wanted to make sure that I didn't miss too many who should be playing because it's difficult to get to all the places, and cover all the angles especially at the start. That's all I set myself. You can just do the best you can. If it doesn't go for you, at least you'll know you've given it a good old shot.'

At the outset, he declared his intention to trawl for talent in every county in the Republic. By the end of his first year, there were only six of the 26 counties left unvisited, and in mitigation, he could cite the fact that, during the first 12 weeks of the new job, he spent 33 days looking at players in England. Only around a third of the 92 clubs in England had answered his written request for information about any Irish players they might have, so there was some groundwork that needed to be done over there.

'I started flying to matches in England. I'd hang around afterwards and at this stage, I've built up a reasonable relationship with a few clubs where there's a good gang of Irish. It's about give and take with the clubs and I don't always get what I want. The clubs are happy that their players are getting international experience but they're not always happy that their fellas are going away because it's not convenient. I think they'd like the matches to be played in the middle of the night in the summer when there's no danger of them getting injured.'

The logistics of a Dublin-based manager travelling to Britain every week to scrutinise prospects may soon be complicated further. Since taking up this job, reports have reached Kerr about the talented sons of expatriate Irishmen and women growing up in locations as diverse as Italy and Denmark. Thinking about it, he laughs at the fact that pretty soon, the FAI may have to significantly extend his travel budget. The emigration of the '70s and '80s flung the Irish all over Europe and an inevitable by-product of this is that one or two of the next batch of second generation players are as likely to hail from somewhere like Copenhagen as Cricklewood.

For the moment, he alleviates his present workload by enlisting the help of Ian Evans, the Irish Under-21 manager. Working from London, Evans has a large number of venues within striking distance of his home, and every so often, Kerr will fax him a list of possible candidates whom he might be able to cast an eye over.

'We might have one player each at Norwich, Wimbledon or Swansea and it's not practical for me to go there and watch one boy because when I go there, he mightn't even be playing which is immensely frustrating. Ian Evans picks up a lot for me in the south of England so a lot of the matches I have been going to are in the North. The ideal thing for me is if say, Everton's As and Bs are playing at home against Tranmere Rovers and Liverpool where we'd have lots of fellas too.

'There was one morning this season when it worked out like that. Between the two games at Everton's training ground, there were 11 Irish playing. Bellfield is an L-shaped complex so if you stand at an angle between both corner flags, it's possible to keep one eye on each game. It's difficult to do that but at least they're all in the one place.'

Inevitably, it doesn't always work out like that. On another Saturday morning, Kerr rushed to a Sheffield Wednesday versus Nottingham Forest youths game because there was the possibility of five Irish togging out. When he got there, only two had made the cut, and Alan Quinn, the player he had come specifically to see, wasn't one of them.

'I was cracking up looking at the match, thinking Quinn was better than what was out on the field. I was steaming about it, thinking there was 20 other matches I could have been at that day that would have been more useful. Then a couple of weeks later, the young fella ends up playing in the first team. I said to him: "Quinner, when I went over to see you, you weren't even in the youths team." "I know," he says. "I got a couple of games for the reserves, played great, and he brought me in." '

Kerr could claim a significant part in the rise of Alan Quinn. In conversation with a Sheffield Wednesday coach at a Dublin schoolboys league game, Kerr had informed the visitor that Quinn, the best player in his age group in Dublin, wasn't playing. Acting on the tip-off, Wednesday sent a scout to find a game where Quinn was playing, and within five months of arriving at Hillsborough he had made his first team début.

Supremely conscious of his role within the domestic game, Kerr doesn't stint either when it comes to attending matches in Ireland, and his record so far is 11 separate fixtures in two days. 'It involves a fair bit of dashing here and there but I remember sitting down on the Monday morning after that weekend, thinking about the 300 or so players I'd seen and wondering if somebody asked me then about the outside right of such and such a team, could I answer? I was trying to work out a picture in my head of every player, having only seen maybe half an hour of the game he was in. But I was quite happy that I could do it.

'It's kind of mad and you don't need to do it like that but that's the way I wanted it to be. Like most jobs, you can find work if you really want to, or you can say, "Well, we've no match for a month now, I'll take it easy." I could take the handy way out and just go to a match on a Saturday afternoon or I could watch the match on the telly on Sunday rather than try to go to five different games.

'But I understand fellas running schoolboy teams around the country, I know the scrapping that goes on, the dedication and the voluntary work. That's why I like to get to as many matches as I can so that fellas can say, "Well at least he came and had a look at our fellas." I think that's important. I know how much I appreciated it if somebody came to watch my schoolboy team playing, even if we never got anybody near an international team, I know it meant a lot.

'I wish I could get to more games every week because I know what it was like when I was running schoolboy teams and even League of Ireland teams and nobody seemed to care. There didn't seem to be any relationship between me running Crumlin United in the schoolboys league for eight or nine years and what the international team was all about.'

Kerr feels that he has other responsibilities too with this job. Having watched a game in England, he will always dally to have words with the Irish boys who were involved. He'll know from talking to the coaches at the clubs which ones are settling in best and which ones are having problems, and he always feels obliged to offer some comfort to those for whom the dream may not be living up to expectations.

'I would always try and look at the positive angle for a fella. I'd say: "Hang in there, the reason that you're over here is because you are one of the best players around. You came from Ireland because they wanted you badly. You were a very, very good player at home, and you have to transfer that here. You have to show them in every training session, you have to do your best, play to the limit and they're going to have to play you because it will come around for you."

'I might console a fella too by telling him that he's a year younger than the rest of them and that he has a year to go, so it's not such a big thing that he's not in the team. I always find something to tell them but there is definitely an element of sadness when it's not going right. You can see it in their eyes the moment that you get there.'

Throughout his years at St Pat's, Kerr had regular contact with the game in England but since plunging himself into the world of youths football, he has seen at close hand the iniquities of professional football, and most specifically how they impact on the vast numbers of Irish players trying to make their name in a foreign land. Even the numbers tell a story. Back when he was assistant to Liam Tuohy, Kerr remembers that if a player was at an English club, it was almost taken for granted that he'd be selected in the international squad for the relevant age group. But that was when there was maybe a dozen eligible for Ireland in each age batch. All that has changed.

'For the team that we took to the European Under-16 championships, we had 25 that were eligible from England and Scotland and we only ended up with nine of those in the squad. From that, I can see that there's an awful lot of fellas going over there that are too afraid of missing out on something but really just aren't good enough. They're all seeing England and Scotland as the place now and they're wrong.

'With what's going on in football, there really is no sense in the clubs having eight or ten Irish fellas. How many of the Irish lads at Celtic are ever going to play in the first team? When the next guy comes in after Wim Jansen, what's he going to do? He'll change around a couple of foreigners for another couple, that's what. He's not going to bring in the lad in the reserves who's 20 and who's been scoring a lot of goals. That just doesn't seem to work anymore.

'George Graham has done it at Leeds. He saw the fellas doing well, and he gave Alan Maybury and Stephen McPhail a bit of a go in the first team, and he also had Gary Kelly and Ian Harte in there. But I don't think that can go on because at the end of the summer, they are going to have ten Irish kids there and where are they going to go? Those boys are getting a good football education all right but are they going to make it? How many of them?

'The honesty and logic of that, I have a problem with. Somebody in there has to say: "Hold on, why are we doing this? What are we doing and are we really being honest about it?" It's a great opportunity if they get in but the way the game is going, they will have to have a realistic look at that, everybody does. There are clubs now with all these Irish kids there, and there's going to be more and more of it going on.'

Unsurprisingly, Kerr feels that an Irish teenager has a better chance if he signs for a smaller, less fashionable club than if he becomes the latest addition to one of the burgeoning Irish colonies like the one at Elland Road. In the constant desperation not to miss out on the next great Irish talent, the English clubs seem to put quantity over quality, hoping that by snaffling up ten good youngsters, they might happen upon one great. Good business for them but not so for those who have to make up the fodder.

'I'd be questioning clubs' judgement on some of the fellas that they take. There's a couple of very big clubs who have Irish lads and I'd be looking at them, thinking they have no chance. I'd watch a game and say to myself: "This boy has no chance of being a first team player at this club unless my own judgement is way wrong." That saddens me because it's not a very nice environment to be in. In some of the cases, I think it's actually the parents being on an ego trip. The parents want to be able to go into the pub and say that their son is away at an English club. But really, the life is not very nice and it's not a very natural environment compared to going to school here.

'It's a tough enough life going to school here, trying to get your Inter Cert and your Leaving. While we didn't like it when we were kids and we thought it was quite restrictive with our parents telling us when to come in and come out, it's worse over in England. They don't allow boys out after ten at night, and they even have people ringing up at half ten to check that they're in.

'When I was a kid, I'd have loved to have gone away to England and been a player. But I know that I would not have been able to survive because I would have died if somebody abused me or slagged me. I would have suffered because I wasn't very confident and brash but there's none of us really like that. You can put on this outer skin of ego but really inside you're not sure. With kids, there isn't great confidence there and it can be so difficult in that environment.

'At the football clubs, they're all walking around in their flash gear, and they have different accents and big reputations and they're shouting orders at the kids. They're trying to keep everyone in their place because football is the most insecure business. Everybody is looking over their shoulders and they have to be seen to be authoritative in whatever little section they work because they never know when the manager is going to change. When you see the jobs they have to do, and the way they're treated, it's not a very natural environment for kids.

'Some of the clubs are very nice to them but it's still a hard life compared to living at home, having your mates and going to school with all the banter. Coming home from Oporto recently after we won the trophy, there was a few of them walking behind coming through the airport. I heard Barry Quinn saying: "It's always great to be coming back into the airport." Then I think it was Alan Quinn saying: "Yeah, but it's brutal when you're coming back out here knowing that you're going back there." That's the reality of it, and yet they're all bursting to go.'

Close proximity to two generations of Ireland's best young footballers affords Kerr a unique view of just why they are so sought after by British clubs. It used to be almost all about their raw talent but lately, he thinks that has shifted a little. 'One of the things that I hear them saying about our boys is that they're lovely lads, terribly well-mannered kids, and they seem to have a special bit of hunger about them because they've had to fight to get where they are. I often hear the English coaches saying too that they seem to come from very good backgrounds, that the parents are lovely people. I think because they're from very stable backgrounds that makes them courteous and well-mannered and less likely to be messers, maybe. That's a huge change from what they thought of us in general, years ago.'

The increased numbers playing soccer in Ireland is the legacy of Jack Charlton's success but Kerr has harvested it like no other. Establishing the secret of his success isn't an exact science but people who have worked with him can give pointers. Most often, they say that it's the obsessive way he prepares for games which makes the difference. As St Pat's prepared for a crucial away game towards the end of their 1996 title-winning season, Kerr asked their chief executive Pat Dolan to have a fleet of cars following the team bus just in case it broke down and they'd be late. No point in taking chances.

The attention to detail came with him to the Ireland scene. A couple of weeks before he took the Under-20s to Malaysia, he had them working out in Limerick with their training jackets on in order to simulate the humidity and heat they would experience in the Far East. Even on the afternoon before his Under-16 team won the European championships, Kerr had a difference of opinion with his assistant, Noel O'Reilly, about just what time they should leave the team hotel for the ground, 5.10 or 5.20 p.m.?

There are other nuggets too. Those who have seen the considerate way in which he deals with players who may be surplus to requirements have been astonished because football is not renowned as a caring profession. 'I don't believe in cutting somebody off and being ruthless about it. I don't believe in bringing them up the hard way. Let them down the hard way and they'll be all the better for it. It isn't the way I'd like them to be with me and I'd hope that any fella that ever left Pat's would think the same.'

The humane qualities are only the half of his talent. The next step is ensuring that the passion which informs his own attitude to the game is imparted to his players with obvious results. 'If you can identify the little bit of torch that starts them and then let the flame spread; if you can just find the angle to get the inspiration, then you'll see that there's certainly a lot of passion about the fellas. Finding it isn't that hard for me. There's always an angle in every match, always an angle to touch a fella's, I don't know, is it his soul or his patriotism, whatever?

'When a group is together, it's important to identify some spark that brings out some real team spirit. To some degree it's easier with an international team because the matches aren't so frequent, and you don't have to bring it up again. It's different from doing it with a club where you can't say the same things every week. You can only use the same lines so often. With the international team, you're fresh, you're a different voice to what they're used to. You talk differently to the fellas that talk to them every week.

'The whole thing is different, you talk to them about different things, and the players they're playing with are different players to the ones they're used to playing with. They don't develop any great jealousies or tensions either like they would at club level. It's a strange thing professional football. The fellas who should be your best mates in the club are actually the fellas who are stopping you going on and progressing, the fellas who are going to stop you getting a job.'

Noel O'Reilly has described the way in which their teams have had success as being down to a combination of 'passion and panache' and certainly, the young players representing Kerr's teams do seem to combine a Trojan work ethic with a brand of genuinely attractive football. When they don't have the ball, he urges them from the sideline to: 'Get it and play'. When they do have it, he lets them express themselves. It seems the perfect blend of flair and fortitude.

'After the Norway match last year, when we won 3-0, Tuohy told me that it was the best he'd seen from an Irish team for many a year. I said: "Ya bollix, you mean it's the best you've seen since you were managing the team yourself." But I was worried because I wanted it to look right for him. He always liked the team to look right, for there to be a few little fellas playing who could do a few tricks. He'd understand the pragmatism of it as well though. He wouldn't be short of saying: "Just sit in and get the rosary beads out and hope for the best." When it came to the team, he was always pragmatic.'

Kerr's ongoing search for the best young players in the

country brought him to Home Farm in 1998 to see an Under-17 game. 'There was an Under-9 match going on to my right with all these parents shouting and roaring, and there's Tuohy away to the right coaching the team. And I'm thinking "My God, the people involved in that Under-9 game probably don't understand the greatness of this man." Anyway, after the game, he came up to watch the 17s team and we started talking.

'I said: 'The centre-half is missing from Home Farm," and he says: "Yeah, he got a kick in the other match last Sunday." Immediately, he'd have known everything about the Under-17 team and then he'd be able to say to me "Did you see the little lad on the right wing with the Under-9s?" The enthusiasm he has for it is something else. I would hope to be like that when I'm his age and to have enjoyed it as much too. But I could never be like him, he was a one-off.'

Ten days after his team had made history in Scotland, Brian Kerr picked up the phone to hear Liam Tuohy's voice at the other end. Kerr knew that Tuohy had been away on holiday, and realised the call would come as soon as he returned. 'He told me that he watched the match in The Hogan Stand in Palma Nova with a gang of fellas, and that it was so great, it brought tears to his eyes. I was on the other end, thinking "I'll have that. That'll do me." '

Chapter Ten

Career on a knife edge

The blade tore through his jersey, punctured the skin, ruptured an artery leading to one of his kidneys, and came to rest three quarters of an inch from his heart. At first, there was no pain. Just a shortness of breath, an inability to suck in enough air to stave off the oncoming shock. After that, he remembers only the babble of voices swirling around him as he lay on the kitchen floor. He can't recall telling the young garda about the fact that he was supposed to be going to Arsenal. Doesn't know who cut the Ireland jersey he was wearing from his back. Doesn't remember much, doesn't particularly want to.

This wasn't one of those jerseys that are available to buy in the shops. It was authentic, replete with the number ten stitched into the front and back. His number 10. Vincent Butler, the manager of the Irish Under-15s handed it to him in a dressing-room in Wales three months earlier. His first game for his country. So many people asked him for the jersey afterwards, but his father kept telling him he should hold on to his first, that it was special. The jersey is still the property of the gardai, an exhibit in the case against the boy accused of stabbing Declan Field on 3 January 1998.

For Declan Field, representing Ireland was one more step on the road to playing professional football in England. Ask him how he played for the Irish team in Fishguard that day, and he replies: 'All right, I was a bit nervous.' Other observers say he was Ireland's man of the match. 'He was comfortably the best player on the field,' says Vincent Butler. 'All going well, he would have been an ever-present in the team for all of this season. He would have been starting every game in the middle of midfield. He's not as physically strong as other lads but he makes up for that with skill. He's creative and constructive, he sees things that other players just don't see.' In other words, he is a number 10.

Butler qualifies his praise with the addendum that he might be a bit biased, but too many independent judges have been seduced by Field's talent for that to be the case. At the age of 11, he won the All Ireland soccer skills competition, and as soon as he turned 12, the representatives of English clubs were beating a path to his door. Millwall headed the queue back then. Four times, they had him over to the New Den to train, and they urged him to sign, even though he wasn't old enough. By the time he was, they were no longer alone in courting his signature. Blackburn, West Ham United, Sunderland and Arsenal were all on the scent too.

Blackburn sent him a contract that lies unsigned in a cupboard in his house, and he actually played for West Ham in the Northern Ireland Youths Tournament, The Milk Cup, alongside Joe Cole, the most talked-about young apprentice in the English game. Still, it was Arsenal who won the day. Liam Brady called in one afternoon at the Field's home in Darndale, north Dublin, and that was enough to swing it their way. Declan's mother likes to mock his father about his being so unnerved by Brady's presence that he could barely pour the coffee into the visitor's cup. His father counteracts that Brady made them all feel very at ease. Declan just says: 'I knew they were a very good club for me.'

Shortly after his 15th birthday in July 1997, he committed himself to Arsenal. The club gave him the option of moving across immediately or waiting a year, and he decided he could do with the extra time. His parents agreed that 12 more months would mature him, and ultimately make him better equipped to cope with his new career. Having left school, he began working part-time in a printing factory and continued to play for Belvedere Boys.

Arsenal made arrangements so he would spend several weeks in England during the season, acclimatising to the life, and having been over to Highbury in October, he was due to fly to London again on 5 January for more training. Forty-eight hours before he was supposed to leave, he was stabbed in the stomach with an eight-inch chef's knife.

Bernard and Jackie Field were in bed when their son came in, asking them if he could stay over in a friend's house. This was a regular enough occurrence, and as soon as they had established that the parents of the other boy were present, there was no problem. Declan left the house, wearing his beloved orange Ireland jersey, and carrying a copy of the video *Mortal Kombat*. Two hours later, Jackie Field sat in an ambulance, clutching her son's hand, listening to him moaning, and watching black liquid oozing from the wound in his belly.

With a court case still pending, how Declan Field came to be stabbed in the kitchen of the house where he was staying cannot be reported but the suffering and anguish his family went through can.

The Fields only heard the last part of what the garda on their doorstep was saying to their eldest son: 'Hurry, this is serious.' They both jumped into their clothes but Bernard had to stay to mind the younger kids. He picked up the phone and rang his brothers, and as soon as they arrived, he ran to the house where the incident happened. By the time he got there, Declan was being carried out on a stretcher to the ambulance. 'I knew when he wouldn't talk back to me that this was really serious.'

For five hours, Bernard and Jackie Field sat in the waiting room. 'They told us that they had to operate immediately and in Beaumount Hospital that night, we didn't know whether he was alive or dead,' says Jackie Field. 'A young guard came in though, and told me that Declan had been telling him all about going to Arsenal as he lay on the kitchen floor so that made me feel better. But it wasn't until six o'clock the next morning that the doctors told us he was alive but critical. They removed one of his kidneys in the operation, and his pancreas was also messed up.'

Once their son was out of danger, the Fields used to measure his recovery in terms of how many tubes were taken out of his body each day. The less tubes, they felt, the better he was getting. That still didn't make it any easier to cope. Jackie Field broke down one morning while ironing a clean shirt that Declan had asked her to bring to the hospital. 'It just hit me then looking at the shirt,' she says, 'how near my boy came to dying.'

During the two weeks he spent in hospital, Declan had good days and bad. The first time he walked after the operation, he got a round of applause from all the other patients in his ward. Then there was the afternoon that Liam Brady called in, causing a minor stir. The older patients were all asking him: 'Is it all right if we call you Liam, Mr Brady?' Brady brought with him chocolates and an assurance from Arsenal that nothing had changed. Once he regained full fitness, they still wanted him to be their player. There are, Brady told Declan, plenty of full-time pros with only one kidney.

On another occasion, Bernard Field arrived at the hospital to find his son slumped in a chair, crying. 'He was depressed because somebody had been in to visit, and they had told him about all the different tournaments with Ireland that he was going to miss out on because of this. I tried to console him by saying: "After this, you'll have your whole career ahead of you." But it was hard for him to think like that at the time.'

The hospital staff were especially sympathetic. They had been aware of his budding football career from the start. After all, when he came round following the operation, the first thing he said to the nurse tending him was: 'Will I still be able to go to Arsenal?'

The scar from his operation stretches almost from his breastbone down to his navel. It itches less than it used to, but the only way he can scratch it is with the palm of his hand, through his shirt. For a while the tenderness of the scar made it impossible for him to sleep on that side. If the wound is no longer sore to touch, he does worry about how it will stand up to a lifetime's jostling for a football.

When he entered hospital, Declan weighed 9st 6lb. Shortly after he left, he had dipped under 8st. The greatest battle of his fledgling professional career should have been proving he was a better footballer than his peers at Highbury. Instead, his first major obstacle will be to regain and retain the weight he has lost.

'I reassured Declan that as far as we are concerned, he could still play football, and all he had to do was prove that to us,' says Liam Brady. 'He does need to build himself up weight-wise, he lost a lot of weight and he wasn't the biggest of boys in the first place. He has to do some serious developing as regards eating the right things, and putting on strength, but Declan is a very good player and we didn't want to lose him.

'I might be a little bit biased towards somebody like Declan. I see some of myself in him. I always remember that there were a few doubts about me because of my size so I don't let size come into it. They used to have me on the Complan diet one time at Arsenal to build me up.' Those who have seen Field play say the resemblance with the teenage Brady isn't just restricted to the similarity of build.

For Bernard and Jackie Field, the weight issue required a huge change of tack. Whereas before the stabbing, they would berate Declan for eating four bowls of cereal in a row, they now had to start bending his ear about the need to stuff his face. The doctors prescribed him a diet sheet, full of foods he wasn't exactly fond of. That 'chipper dinners' were his favourite meal is one more similarity with the Brady who went by the nickname of 'Chippy' for the same reason.

The February morning that I called to the Field household, Declan was able to put on his favourite jeans for the first time since the incident without them hanging loose off his hips, and his mother was enthused by this. The Fields were trying to concentrate on the positives like that because the negatives were only getting them down too much.

'This has put an enormous strain on us,' said Jackie. 'When I walk past that house where it happened, it makes me feel sick like, you know, the way you feel sick when you're nervous. I feel like that every time I walk past that house. It's an unbelievable situation. I know that it's happening to me but sometimes I actually think it's happening to somebody else.'

Her husband was equally perplexed by it all. 'I don't know what the situation is with Declan's health long-term. He looks all right now, and hopefully it's good. But this great chance he's been given of a career in football has been definitely jeopardised by all this.'

Two days after this interview, Declan went to see his Irish team-mates training before their departure for a tournament in Portugal. It was a journey he should have been making too, and seeing them off, he could only think about how a player must play in all the internationals in a season to qualify for receiving a commemorative cap. Declan will have to wait another year for the chance to pick up the Irish cap he has dreamt about.

The file regarding the case is still with the Director of Public Prosecutions, Declan Field's beloved Ireland jersey is with the gardai and in July 1998, he was due to begin his professional career at Highbury. After the nightmare has ended, the dream lives on.

Bibliography

A Strange Kind of Glory – Eamon Dunphy, Heinemann, 1991

Fyffes Dictionary of Irish Sporting Greats – John Gleeson, Etta Place, 1993

Ireland on the Ball – Donald Cullen, ELO Publications

Jack Charlton: The Autobiography – Jack Charlton, Partridge Press, 1996

The Boys in Green – Sean Ryan, Mainstream Publishing Co, 1997

The Team That Jack Built – Paul Rowan, Mainstream Publishing Co, 1995

With Heart and Hand – Tom Williams, Blackwater Press, 1996